BORN TO PLEASE

BORN TO PLEASE

Compliant Women / Controlling Men

KAREN BLAKER, PH.D.

St. Martin's Press • New York

BORN TO PLEASE

Copyright © 1988 by Karen Blaker.
All rights reserved. Printed in the United States of
America. No part of this book may be used or
reproduced in any manner whatsoever without
written permission except in the case of brief
quotations embodied in critical articles or reviews.
For information, address St. Martin's Press, 175 Fifth
Avenue, New York, N.Y. 10010

Design by Karin Batten

Library of Congress Cataloging-in-Publication Data

Blaker, Karen.
  Born to please : compliant women/controlling men /
Karen Blaker.
      p.   cm.
    ISBN 0-312-02172-0
    1. Women—Psychology.   2. Assertiveness
(Psychology)
3. Interpersonal relations.   I. Title.
HQ1206.B456   1988
155.6'33—dc19   88-12015
                                                      CIP

First Edition

10 9 8 7 6 5 4 3 2 1

Dedicated to loving relationships
between men and women, based
upon mutual respect.

My most sincere thanks to:

My collaborator, Catherine Whitney
My literary agent, Jane Dystel
My editor, Toni Lopopolo
and WOR Radio

CONTENTS

BORN ᵀᴼ PLEASE

INTRODUCTION

Once upon a time, I loved a man I couldn't please. I lived with him for twenty-one years, had two beautiful children with him, and tried in every way I could to make him happy. But nothing worked.

Now, seven years after the hurt, humiliation, and horror of the divorce, I can honestly say that I am grateful to him. I see now that I was trapped in a pattern of living to please a controlling man. He freed me by becoming increasingly bizarre in his behavior, until I reached a breaking point and walked away to get rid of him. Then a miracle happened: *I found myself, a self I had not realized I'd lost.*

I discovered that I had become so eager to please that I had lost the possibility of real intimacy—the experience of presenting a fully formed, authentic

1

adult self to another person, with all the risk that entails.

I also realized I had developed a type of phobia after so many years of putting others first and myself last. This phobia took the form of an irrational fear of looking at or expressing myself without validation or approval from him. I do believe that this phobia made my marriage worse or, at the very least, caused it to last long after it should have ended. It's not that I blamed myself for the problems so much as I came to accept my part of the responsibility for what I still consider to be a real disaster.

As I worked with women in my private practice and talked with them on my radio call-in advice program on WOR in New York, I began to realize the scope of the problem. That's when I gave my phobia a name. I called it "Me Phobia"—the fear of being myself in my relationship. This fear was deep and complex: He might leave me if I could not be what he wanted. I might be alone. I might feel empty without him. I might fail if I had to make it on my own. And I discovered that, to one degree or another, most women struggle with Me Phobia.

I decided that I would have to help myself before I could offer guidance to other women. So I set out to establish a healing program for myself that would also work for others. My discoveries form the basis of this book. I have found positive, creative ways to begin defining the self that lies underneath all the layers of subservient behavior.

If you follow my guidelines, I know you will begin to feel better about yourself. You may not like the short-term ramifications of the change, especially if it involves the risk of losing everything that has defined you up to this point. But I promise that you will find a more exciting self—your *true* self—and in the process, you will take a big step toward becoming a healthy adult woman.

Is it worth the risk? Only you can answer that question. But before you say no and close this book, I ask you to give me a chance to show you that it's not as hard as you may think to conquer your Me Phobia.

—Karen Blaker, Ph.D.

1

LOVING TO PLEASE

Joan lived most of her days in a fog of apprehension. She loved her husband, George, but his temper ran on a short fuse and when he got angry, he could be very mean. He had never hit her, but once he threw a plate at the wall and barely missed her head.

Lately things had been getting worse. And yet Joan clung to the belief that George really did love her, deep down inside. In many ways, she could even understand his impatience. He was so much smarter!

When they'd met five years earlier, Joan was struggling to make a living at a low-paying secretarial job. George was a client of the firm. He asked her out one night after work and she was impressed with how confident and secure he seemed. He was compassionate too, as she described her mother's death the year before and how she felt orphaned. He really seemed to understand. They dated for several months and when he proposed marriage, she was thrilled that this wonderful man had chosen her.

After they were married, George encouraged Joan to quit her job so she could supervise the building of their dream house. Joan was happy that George trusted her with such a big responsibility and she spent many hours working with the architect, poring over the plans.

When the plans were final, she presented them to him proudly and expected him to be as excited as she was. But as George read, he seemed to grow increasingly agitated and he finally threw the papers down in disgust. "These are all wrong," he cried. "I should have known better than to trust you with this."

Joan felt as though she had been stabbed straight through the heart. "Tell me what's wrong, I'll fix it," she pleaded. But he wouldn't speak to her for the rest of the evening. After two days he finally explained what was wrong with the plans. The changes he wanted seemed minor to Joan, and she was surprised that he had been so upset. But she complied with his requests without comment.

From that point on, Joan was constantly on the lookout for what might set George off. She didn't want him to be angry with her. She couldn't bear the weight of his disappointment. She wanted him to be the warm, compassionate man she had married, and she was determined to make his life happy so he would be that way.

But George was a bully. He kept the threat of his anger alive in their marriage deliberately. This made Joan feel that her own opinions and feelings were worthless. In this way, George controlled her.

* * * *

Arlene met Bill when she was twenty-four years old. Describing the meeting to friends she admitted, "He really swept me off my feet. He's older—forty-six—successful, generous, handsome . . ."

Arlene's friends reminded her that he was also married, but she ignored their warnings. "I know," she said. "But he loves me."

There was little question that Bill was attracted to her. He had been married to Jacquie for twenty-three years and, now that their children were in college, their relationship had grown strained. In contrast to Jacquie, Arlene was a career woman with a good job in public relations. She was young, blond, beautiful, and glamorous.

At the time of their meeting, Arlene was involved with another man, and Bill set out to win her away. He showered her with gifts, took her out for romantic evenings, and never stopped telling her how special she was. As they became more involved, Bill repeatedly asked Arlene to go away with him on short one- or two-day trips, and she happily juggled her work schedule to be with him.

One day Bill said, "I wish you could be with me all the time," and her heart leapt with joy. She believed it was only a matter of time until he asked her to marry him—hadn't he told her he was unhappy with his wife?

"I have to take a three-week trip to Europe," he told her. "Come with me."

"I can't get that much time off work," she demurred.

He put his arms around her. "Money isn't important," he whispered. "We are. Don't worry, I'll take care of you."

So Arlene quit her job and became financially dependent on Bill. She wasn't worried about it because she believed she was going to be his wife.

Six months later, the bloom was fading on the relationship. Arlene began to wonder if Bill really would leave his wife. When she pushed him for a commitment, he made excuses. She was afraid of what might happen to her, but he assured her that she was safe with him.

A year went by. Arlene was still out of a job, still being supported by Bill and still pushing him for a commitment. She was panic-stricken. Without Bill she was nothing. She had built her life around him. But the more she pushed, the more distant he became. He made it clear that if she wanted his attention, she would have to stop talking about commitment. He punished her when she pressured him by withdrawing his affection, and soon Arlene stopped speaking about it altogether. She didn't know what else to do.

Bill was in control. He called all the shots—physically, emotionally, and financially. Arlene relinquished the power to him; she felt helpless to fight him, and he knew it.

Sometimes Sarah thought she was going crazy. She had been dating Tom for a year and she loved him deeply. But often, without warning, he would cut her off, grow cold and withdrawn, and stop talking to her for days at a time. Often it seemed that Tom's silences held accusations she just couldn't understand.

On his birthday she decided to surprise him by arranging a dinner party with eight good friends. She made reservations at his favorite restaurant and asked him to meet her there. She thought he'd be very pleased to find his good friends there, too.

When Tom walked into the restaurant and saw everyone gathered to celebrate his birthday, he acted pleased and greeted his friends warmly. But Sarah, who was accustomed to reading even the smallest signs, noticed the familiar tightening of his jaw as he looked at her. She could tell he wasn't pleased—but why not?

After dinner, Sarah and Tom drove back to his apartment. In the car, he was silent and withdrawn, and when they reached his apartment he immediately turned on the television. Finally Sarah couldn't stand it any longer. "Did you enjoy yourself tonight?" she asked.

"I could have done without the crowd. You know I don't like to have big parties on weeknights. I *do* have to work tomorrow."

"But it's your birthday."

Tom looked at her coldly. "Leave it to you to give me something for my birthday that I don't want." And he returned to watching television.

Sarah was crushed and she started to cry. Tom ignored her and continued to stare at the television. She tried to talk to him again, but he wouldn't listen. Finally, in despair, Sarah gathered her things and went home, where she cried herself to sleep. Why didn't Tom love her more? Why couldn't she make him happy? She tried so hard, but she couldn't seem to please him. She felt worthless.

Tom controlled Sarah with his silence. And she allowed him to push her away and diminish her importance in his life.

These are true stories about controlling men and women who try to please them. The women are engaged in a desperate struggle to satisfy men who control them by withholding love, approval and affection. Longing for love, they let their men call the shots. They do everything they can to make their men happy, and agonize about it when nothing seems to work.

In all cases, they fix the blame on themselves:

- "If only I were smarter, he'd be happier with me."
- "If I really pleased him, he'd want to marry me."
- "If I could find out what he wants, he would love me."

They ask themselves: *What's wrong with me? What does he need that I'm not giving him? How can I please him—get him to smile and show his affection and approval?*

These women need to please so much that their men automatically lean toward using this vulnerability as a means of exerting control. It's an unhappy struggle, a no-win proposition. And it's a disturbingly common scenario.

It is easy to see how women fall into the trap of compliance. When we were little girls we learned that being pleasing to others gained us approval.

While rebellion, independence, and assertive behavior are admired in boys, too many of us as girls
learned that this behavior would get us into trouble.

The message we learned and carried into adult-
hood is: "If I am sensitive and pleasing enough to
others, they will love me and that love will nurture
me and make me feel good about myself."

We become hooked on the approval this shortcut
to love brings and we depend on it more and more
until it is the primary theme of all our relationships—
with friends, parents, teachers, our children, and,
most especially, with our men. We wear a smile as
our badge of honor, our signal that we are not threatening and aggressive.

We try to recreate that good little girl, hoping she
will be accepted and loved. We believe wholeheart-
edly that "the meek will inherit the earth." And, all
too often, we learn that this is a fallacy. Instead of
feeling fulfilled and content, we end up feeling anxious, unhappy and resentful.

But we don't trust these feelings as signals that tell
us something is wrong. We've forgotten how to listen
to our inner voices, the ones that say, *"You don't have
to put up with this." "You deserve to be treated better." "You're a person in your own right. You're doing
nothing wrong."* We've turned off the switch, put our
own desires and needs on the back burner until finally we don't know what we really need or want.
Eventually, we become irrationally fearful of ever
taking the time or energy to look inward. We develop
a full-blown case of Me Phobia.

WHAT IS ME PHOBIA?

Think about yourself for a moment. Can you say that you know yourself well—apart from your relationship with a man? Are you able to voice your needs? Can you ask for the things you want?

If you aren't sure, you may have what I call Me Phobia.

Me Phobia is the irrational fear of getting to know the real you.

Are you afraid of what you might find if you look inside? What if you discover those rebellious feelings that were so dangerous when you were young? What if you discover negative or angry emotions about the man you are with? What if you find that you want to be a different kind of person—one he might not approve of?

It may seem dangerous to look inside and risk the eruption of negative feelings. You believe it's easier and safer to handle your insecurity by hiding your feelings behind a smile and trying harder to please your man. But is it?

Although you may think that you risk less by allowing his needs to dictate your behavior, you are, in fact, risking *more.* Not only is your relationship doomed to failure, but you are sacrificing something even more precious—your *self*, the *real* you. We'll talk more about the dangers of Me Phobia. But first, I want you to answer the following questions to see if you are a woman who has buried her own needs to please a man. Check the ones that are true for you:

THE SIGNS OF ME PHOBIA

— When you're upset, you hide your feelings rather than risk causing a scene.
— When you have a strong opinion, you are easily convinced to change your mind.
— You often feel exhausted, but keep on going anyway.
— You overeat or fail to eat when you are nervous or upset.
— You find it hard to voice your negative feelings—especially, "I'm angry" or "I'm hurt."
— If you have strong emotions about something—either good or bad—your reaction is usually to cry.
— You try to avoid being alone, and you feel anxious or upset when you're on your own for an extended period of time.
— You avoid making decisions—even simple ones—without asking the opinion of others.
— You often act cheerful when you are really sad.
— You believe that you're very good at reading the feelings of other people.
— You are the "rock," the one others depend on to keep things running smoothly.
— There are things you would like to do, but you're putting your plans on hold until a future time when people need you less.
— You avoid making requests when you think they will inconvenience others.
— You feel guilty when you have to say no to others.

If you checked four or more of these statements, you have Me Phobia. Your actions, feelings, and ideas are a reaction to others, rather than a reflection of *you*.

You are a prime candidate for a relationship with a man who has a need to control his woman. He can assume the dominant role, and you will allow it because your focus is on gaining his approval, not on pleasing yourself. His approval, to you, equals love.

THE FEAR OF BEING YOURSELF

When you are the "pleaser" in your relationship with a man, you are motivated by fear. I have spoken to countless women who have described to me the dreadful anxiety that grabs them whenever they think about standing on their own, or doing something their men would not approve of.

This fear is a very real emotion—and it's powerful. It's not a small thing that you can overcome easily. It's very big and it dominates your life if you are Me Phobic.

Think about it for a minute. Imagine being *you* in the relationship with your man and not catering to him so much. What would your fears be?

Maybe you would describe them in these ways:

- "He'll reject me."
- "He'll hate me."
- "He won't approve of me."
- "He'll say I'm selfish."
- "He'll hurt me."
- "He'll be mean to me."

- "He'll choose someone else."
- "He'll leave me."

Deep down inside, you fear punishment and/or abandonment if you cannot please your man.

When Emily called in to my radio advice program, she was clearly distressed and on the verge of tears.

"It seems like my husband and I fight all the time," she told me. "I can't stand the yelling—it makes me feel so bad."

"What do you fight about?" I asked her.

"If I don't do things the way he wants them done, he gets so angry. I try to defend myself—after all, nobody's perfect. But it doesn't seem to work. Nothing works."

"What kinds of things make him angry?"

"Well," she said, "here's an example. His parents were coming over for dinner and he wanted me to make this very elaborate dish to impress them. But I said I couldn't. I work until five and there wasn't enough time for me to get it together. He got really mad and started yelling at me that I was a poor excuse for a wife and not only did he think so, but his parents thought so, too. That kind of thing."

"And this reaction is typical?" I asked.

"Oh, yes," she said wearily. "You know, I should have made that special dish. It would have saved me a lot of trouble. I'd rather do anything than put up with the yelling. It's really awful."

Do as I say or I will punish you. It's a very strong message.

The threat of abandonment is even stronger. Joyce, a woman I interviewed for this book, told me: "When

I was living with Brian, I was divorced, had three children, and was in my early thirties. He used to imply that I was over the hill, that no man would want to take on a woman who had three children. Boy, did I believe that was true! I felt I was a burden to him and I had to make up for it by being especially good to him. And I figured that if I lost him I'd never find anyone else who would love me."

If you don't please me, you will be alone.

Your Me Phobia is based on the belief that as long as you can please your man you will be safe from punishment and abandonment. You will be loved and accepted. Even when things get bad, you think the solution is to try harder, give more, make things better for him.

This book will help you understand why trying to please a controlling man doesn't work. It's your recovery program from Me Phobia, the fear of being yourself—a way for you to begin releasing yourself from the control of a man so you can stand strongly and happily on your own.

AN EIGHT-STEP RECOVERY PROGRAM FROM ME PHOBIA

If you answered "yes" to four or more of the questions earlier in this chapter, you have already laid the groundwork for your recovery. You have admitted that you are controlled by your need to please a man.

Now, let me outline the steps you will have to take

to recover from Me Phobia. This is what we will work on together for the remainder of the book.

Step One

Accept the fact that pleasing does not work. Letting a man control your life will not make you happy.

Step Two

Make a commitment to conquer your Me Phobia and free yourself from the control of the man in your life.

Step Three

Review your love relationship to identify the ways you have allowed your man control over you.

Step Four

Examine your past to discover how you have become so vulnerable to the control of a man. Were you the child who won approval by being the most obedient in your family?

Step Five

Understand the typical stages of a relationship between a controlling man and a pleasing woman—and see why these relationships are bound to fail.

Step Six

Face why you stay in a bad relationship and what finally causes you to reach a "breaking point."

Step Seven

Anticipate the "pseudo solutions" in the process of your recovery—the traps you may fall into as you struggle to reach a new understanding of yourself as an individual.

Step Eight

Learn to live and love, free from the control of men, and discover the happiness and strength that comes from being yourself.

$$2$$

HOW PLEASING WRECKS YOUR LIFE

Judy came to see me because she couldn't get over her feelings of hurt and betrayal since the breakup of her relationship with Eric.

"When I met him, I was working as a salesgirl in a department store. Eric was a partner at a prestigious law firm. At the time, I was feeling kind of down on myself for a lot of reasons. I didn't like my job, but I didn't know what else I could do. Eric changed all that. He made me feel so appreciated—like a princess.

"When I told Eric I felt inadequate about being just a salesgirl and not having an important career, he said he liked me the way I was. He used to tell me, 'I can't stand aggressive women. I'm glad you're not one of them.'

"He flattered me and told me how soft and feminine I was. When I moved in with him, he encouraged me to quit my job altogether. He said he didn't want his woman to have to work.

"So I quit and I did a little modeling on the side and worked on my tan and made a nice home for him. But then things started changing in our relationship and sometimes when we fought he'd get nasty and say things like, 'Why can't you be more like so-and-so,' referring to some professional woman who was just the opposite of what he had told me he wanted.

"When I reminded him that he always said he hated that in women, he just looked at me with disgust, as though I had completely missed some big point. In the end, I found out that he was having an affair with a woman lawyer. I had done exactly what he said he wanted, but it sure backfired on me! Now I don't know what to think."

I sympathized with Judy's misery and confusion and I understood why she felt betrayed. She had tried to be everything Eric said he wanted in a woman and yet he had rejected her.

The first step in the recovery from Me Phobia is this: *Accept the fact that pleasing does not work.* It does not guarantee you love or approval. In fact, it almost always backfires.

There are several reasons why living to please a controlling man will not make you happy or secure.

1. PLEASING DOES NOT WORK BECAUSE IT MAKES YOU VULNERABLE TO A CONTROLLING MAN.

In your relationship with a controlling man, he is the actor and you are the *re*actor. He calls the shots and you obey, confident that the more you please him, the more approval you receive and the more he will love you.

But pleasing this kind of man inevitably leads to rejection because it is control he is after, not love. Once he controls you enough to see that you try to please him even when he changes the rules at random, he loses respect for you and rejects you.

This man can work a very dangerous "head trip" on you. He tells you what he wants and then turns his back on you when you give it to him. You blame yourself, thinking you read him wrong, you didn't understand, or that you must try harder.

Deborah met Alan at a party and they hit it off immediately. They ended up spending the entire evening together and Deborah was thrilled when Alan took her phone number and said he would call.

They went out the following weekend and Deborah was very moved by Alan's stories of his difficult childhood. His father had died when he was very young and his mother was forced to work long hours outside the home. Alan and his brother fended for themselves most of the time.

"I was so jealous of my friends who had their mothers at home," Alan told her. "I missed not having home-cooked meals and cookies in the oven. I guess now I'm looking for the kind of woman who will be there for me."

Deborah felt great tenderness for Alan after he admitted this. She thought he had missed a lot of nurturing in his childhood and he craved it now. That was fine with her because she loved being a nurturer.

Alan and Deborah fell into a comfortable pattern of behavior. He shared with her his hopes, dreams, and struggles at work; she was supportive and understanding, even when he became moody and withdrew from her. Their relationship went along smoothly for several months.

Then one weekend Deborah invited him to her apartment for an intimate home-cooked dinner—the kind that he loved. But Alan called her the day before and said, "I can't come to dinner. I have so much work to do and I'm going to hole up in my apartment and finish it. I guess I'll have a pizza brought in or something."

Alan sounded so forlorn that Deborah's heart went out to him. She devised a plan. She would make a very special casserole and carry it to him so he would at least have a good dinner.

"I took this great meal over to his apartment and rang the bell. It really made me feel good to be doing this for him. But when he opened the door and I presented him with my casserole, he was very cool. In fact, he was like a different person. He let me know by his attitude that I had made a big mistake, but for the life of me I couldn't figure out what I'd done wrong. When I called him the next day, he indicated that he didn't appreciate surprise visits. I told him I didn't understand, because everything he had said to me before had led me to believe that he needed some tender, loving care. Besides, by that time, we had grown quite close so I didn't see anything wrong with the gesture. But he was very cool to me for a long time, like I had crossed an invisible line."

You can't win when you try to please a controlling man. You never get it just right and your self-confidence is pulled out from under you like someone was playing a cruel prank on you. You are bound to be abused and it is likely that you will be left—or that the situation will become so intolerable that you will be the one forced to leave.

2. PLEASING DOES NOT WORK BECAUSE YOU NEVER GET TRUE APPROVAL FROM HIM.

When you *do* get positive feedback from the man in your life, it isn't *you* he is admiring but how good you are at being who he wants you to be. It is not real acceptance—it is applause for a good performance. And it's easy to get hooked on that applause because it feels so good to win his praise. In the long run, however, it only accentuates your Me Phobia because you try harder and harder to please him and never really learn about your own needs.

When I interviewed women for this book, nearly all of them admitted to changing something important in their lives for their controlling men. One woman said that for ten years she wore her hair in a style that she absolutely hated because that was how he liked it. Another talked of giving up her lifetime ambition to be a musician because he disapproved. Still another reported, "Every time I went out I had to parade in front of him to get his approval on what I was wearing. If I was going somewhere without him, he would insist that I dress conservatively. When I went out with him he wanted me to look sexy. I complied."

Being a "good girl" and receiving his approval feels good. All of us love to hear, "You look wonderful," or "You're so supportive," or all the different ways a man says, "You're doing what makes me happy."

But the approval is false and the stakes only get higher. I have a friend who prided herself on looking terrific and her husband showered her with compliments. She concentrated on keeping her body perfect for him and he was always showing her off at parties. That worked fine until she discovered a malignant lump in her breast and had to have a mastectomy— he couldn't control that. They divorced soon after.

Trying to please a controlling man never wins you *real* approval or healthy love. It only undermines your self-respect.

3. PLEASING DOES NOT WORK BECAUSE IT LIMITS YOUR CAPACITY TO ACCEPT LOVE.

Every controlling man tries, at times, to meet your needs. But if you have blinders on because you are focused only on pleasing him, you will either not notice or will reject his small gestures because a pleaser has trouble accepting love. Since you don't reinforce his positive behavior, he will eventually stop trying and resort to being even more controlling. Where at first he might shower you with gifts or bring you flowers, eventually he will stop trying to win your pleasure and simply demand it.

Both Albert and Rhonda worked very hard at their jobs, and Albert knew that it wasn't fair for Rhonda to be responsible for all the housework, too. But whenever he tried to help, she criticized him. He washed the dishes and she showed him the water spots. He vacuumed the carpets and she pointed out the areas he'd missed. Whenever he tried to help, she found fault and eventually he stopped making an effort. Rhonda longed for Albert's support, but she was afraid to let him too far inside her world.

In a different story, Linda had always deferred to Robert's opinion on everything—from the way she fixed her hair to the way she decorated their home. One year they had saved several thousand dollars to take a special vacation. Linda went out and got travel brochures and they talked about all the different places they could go.

"These all sound fine," Robert told her. "Why don't you pick a place where you'd like to go."

"You must have a preference," Linda said.

"Not really. I'll be happy just to get away."

Linda was at a loss. She was afraid that she might choose a vacation that Robert would not enjoy and he would blame her. She nagged and nagged until finally he became angry and threw up his hands. "Okay, let's just go to Hawaii."

Linda was relieved that Robert had made the decision, but she was disappointed because she'd hoped he would choose Europe. By deferring to him, she sacrificed her own preference. She also reinforced Robert's controlling behavior, since he saw that life was much easier if he just took charge.

This may be a painful thing for you to face, but when you live in fear of displeasing your man, you severely limit your own receptiveness to love and caring.

4. PLEASING DOES NOT WORK BECAUSE IT EVENTUALLY CAUSES YOU TO LOSE CONTROL.

When Joanne came into my office, her face looked haggard with worry and her eyes were red from crying. "I don't know what's happening to me," she sobbed. "I used to be so easygoing and calm. Now, all I ever do is scream. James is right when he says I'm a bitch but I don't know how to stop it."

"Why are you so angry?" I asked her gently.

"I don't know." She shook her head as if to deny that she was angry. "Things aren't so bad . . . I love James. It just seems that lately I blow up over nothing. Then James will say, 'You bitch . . . get off my back,' and I'll cry for hours. It's a nightmare."

"Can you give me any examples of the things that make you blow up?"

"Usually, it's just little things, like James coming home late from the office without calling, or his criticizing me in some way. Never anything big. I can see I'm behaving in an unreasonable way."

Like most compliant women, Joanne wanted desperately to be in control of her negative feelings—she thought they were bad. Since her focus had always been on avoiding conflict (what she called being "easygoing"), she had never dealt with handling anger in herself or others. She thought she could control the emotions so that nothing unpleasant would ever happen.

We talked for a while more and I learned that James was a chronic breaker of promises who could not be relied upon to show up when and where he had promised. Whenever Joanne confronted him, he turned the focus back on her, calling her a nag and a bitch. Joanne was frightened of her anger and felt that her feelings were invalid. She came to see me because she wanted help in getting rid of her anger. "If I can just learn to deal with this, I know things will be better between us," she said, blind to the truth.

The truth is that all of us have emotions that include anger. Even if you are concentrating on pleasing your man, you're going to feel these emotions. But they're going to scare you because long ago you probably disowned them as being dangerous.

When feelings are forced underground, they are harder to manage because you never know what is happening with them. When something triggers a release of negative emotions, you feel frightened and depressed.

Being a pleaser does not give you control over negative emotions. Nor does it allow you to recognize that sometimes your anger is valid. You believe that everything that goes wrong is your fault because you cannot control your negative feelings.

"I overreact to things and it causes a lot of problems with my boyfriend," Ella told me. I asked her to describe an instance when she overreacted; she told me the following story.

"We were out drinking with a couple of friends and Charlie was getting pretty high. He started necking with my girlfriend right there at the table. At first, I tried to be a good sport and laughed it off—like, 'Isn't he funny when he gets drunk?' But they kept at it longer than they should have and I started feeling very humiliated and upset. I tried to say something and he laughed at me and went back to what he was doing. Finally, I just lost control. I couldn't help myself, I started screaming. That stopped him but he was furious. He got up and stormed out.

"Later he telephoned me and I thought he was going to apologize, but it was just the opposite. He started telling me how embarrassed I had made him feel, yelling in front of all those people. He demanded an explanation for my behavior.

"I was speechless. *My* behavior? But when I tried

to tell him how I felt, he acted like I was being totally ridiculous. Finally, he convinced me that it was all my fault that this had happened. I ended up apologizing to him."

Ella suspected that there was something twisted in this logic, but she wouldn't admit it. It was easier for her to concern herself with how to get her behavior back in check. Challenging Charlie's behavior was simply too risky.

Now you know.

- Pleasing does not give you control over bad feelings.
- Pleasing does not make you feel good about yourself.
- Pleasing does not allow you to experience true love.
- Pleasing does not buy you security.

Trying to please a controlling man *does* give you Me Phobia. You focus more and more on him and less on yourself. You live in perpetual anxiety, not knowing what your man will find fault with next. Or how he will test your behavior once again. You live a hollow existence where you scramble hopelessly to fill an emptiness that can only be filled from within.

GET ON WITH YOUR RECOVERY

If you recognize yourself in the examples I've given, you may be feeling very upset right now. Most likely you have mixed feelings. On one hand, you recognize that you've embroiled yourself in a destructive relationship. But on the other hand, you truly fear that you will never be able to break free—you're not strong enough.

You say, "I don't care how bad things are. I'll never be able to face life without him . . . alone!"

Or, "I'm not smart enough to make it on my own."

Or, "He'll never be able to accept me if I change and it will only lead to trouble."

Or, "This is the way I've always been. How can I change now?"

Or, "He's not really asking too much. I just need to learn how to be a little more patient and have a more positive attitude."

Maybe you're also feeling a little bit cheated, thinking, "If only I hadn't been raised to please men, I wouldn't be in this situation. It's society's fault . . . it's my parents' fault."

These thoughts are spinning through your mind and I can understand why. You want things to be different, but you can't yet see the light at the end of the tunnel.

This is a good time to take the second step in your road to recovery. I'm going to ask you to sign the following agreement with yourself. It is a contract that states your willingness to embark on the full recovery program and carry out the recommendations in this book to the best of your ability. When you sign it you are making a promise to yourself that will change your life—if you can follow through with your pledge.

YOUR RECOVERY CONTRACT

I (name) _____
on (date) _____ agree to follow the eight
steps to recovery from Me Phobia to the best of my
ability. I realize that I have a strong need for approval and that I tend to let men control my life. I
also realize that this is not good for me, that I can
never find happiness or real love as long as I allow
this to continue. I want to get to know myself.

(signed) _____

Ask yourself: How do you feel about having
signed this contract? How much hope do you have
for recovery?

Now that you have made this agreement with yourself, you are ready to move on and conquer your Me
Phobia. It won't be easy and it won't happen overnight, but I'll be with you every step of the way.

Let's get started!

3

HOW MEN
CONTROL YOU

You have already completed two steps of the recovery program for Me Phobia. You understand why pleasing doesn't work and you have made a commitment to recover from the Me Phobia that your pleasing behavior has induced.

Step three is the process of reviewing your love relationships. Why do men treat you the way they do? How can they manipulate your emotions so completely? What gives them power over you? Finally, how do your responses help keep the destructive and vicious cycle alive?

As a pleaser, you are particularly attracted to a controlling man. Why? First of all, he seems strong and dependable, at least in the beginning of the relationship. You like the idea that he's so sure of himself because you don't always feel so sure of *yourself.*

Second, he has definite plans for what should be done and when. He issues clear guidelines about what he wants and what are the best ways you can please him. He makes you feel secure in the knowledge that you have only to please him to receive his love.

Finally, you see him as being able to feel and express things that have always been too dangerous for you to admit that you feel. He may be openly aggressive, openly angry, openly competitive and openly self-oriented—all of the things you would secretly like to be but can't. In a vicarious fashion, some of your needs are met when you hook up with him.

You don't recognize his behavior as being controlling at the beginning of the relationship. On the contrary, you find it appealing. You're flattered that he pays so much attention to you. The very qualities that later cause you so much pain are the ones that seduce you in the beginning.

You may ask, "Why does he control me?" That's a good question. Often a man tries to control a woman because it makes him feel more secure when he dominates. Not unlike dictators who control their subjects through fear.

Just as *you* are afraid of being rejected if you assert yourself, *he* is afraid that he will lose you if he doesn't keep you feeling that you are nothing without him.

In addition, he may need his superior position to demonstrate to his friends that he is a "man." It's as if he were saying, "I'm not the kind of sissy who has to call home if I'm going to be late for dinner. She'll put it on the table when I'm ready. I'm in control of this relationship." When his friends see him as strong, he can feel powerful.

The controlling man chooses the pleaser because he can tell right away that you are willing to assume the inferior position, that you will expect little and put up with a lot. He will test how far he can go and will find that since you don't have great confidence in yourself, he won't have much trouble keeping you in line. *He can sense your fear of rejection.* It makes him feel safer. He is in control.

You are the victim. He is the bully. And in the same way that a bully terrorizes his victim to prove his strength, your man uses controlling maneuvers to maintain his power over you.

"But he's not that bad," you might protest. "He's not a bully. I please him because I *want* to." Sometimes control is exercised in very subtle ways and you may have chosen to ignore the signs.

If you're not sure where you and your mate stand, answer the questions in the following quiz. Write "Yes" when you feel that the description is usually or always true. Answer "No" when it is not usually or never true.

QUIZ: HOW CONTROLLING IS YOUR MAN?

1. When there's a problem in the relationship, he blames you __.
2. He sometimes drinks too much and becomes physically or verbally abusive __.
3. You know or suspect that he has been involved with other women __.

4. He is late or stands you up for appointments or dates __.
5. He forbids or criticizes your outside activities and hobbies __.
6. He embarrasses you in front of other people __.
7. He gets angry when you disagree with him __.
8. He accuses you of flirting with other men when you are not __.
9. He follows you to check up on you __.
10. He is critical of the way you look or dress __.
11. He insists on driving the car when you go out __.
12. He has hit you __.
13. He does or says things that you never thought you could tolerate __.
14. He stops talking to you or withdraws his affection when he wants to win an argument or make a point __.
15. He says he needs his "freedom" or "space" __.
16. He has pushed you or twisted your arm or used some other physical act to make you bend to his will __.
17. He doesn't allow you to have a checking account, and gives you an allowance to pay the bills __.
18. He uses sex to quiet your doubts about the relationship __.
19. He is not interested in your day __.
20. He gives you extra money or buys you presents when you have been "good" __.
21. He calls you a nag or accuses you of stirring up trouble if you want to talk about the problems in the relationship __.
22. He never calls you by your real name—he uses a demeaning or derogatory nickname __.
23. He doesn't phone when he is going to be late __.

24. He wants you around when he is there __.
25. He has been arrested at least once __.
26. He feels uncomfortable or gets angry with you when you get the attention (because of some aspect of your work or a special accomplishment) __.
27. He puts down your accomplishments __.
28. He trivializes or makes fun of your feelings __.
29. He often says you're too critical __.
30. He flirts with women in front of you __.
31. He makes you feel sorry for him __.
32. He frightens you with threats __.
33. He finds fault with your friends and the people you are close to __.

If you answered yes to twenty or more, your man is very controlling.

If you answered yes to twelve or more, your man is quite controlling.

If you answered yes to five or more, your man is somewhat controlling.

Note that the more controlling your man is, the more of a pleaser you probably are—otherwise you would leave the relationship.

Now, it is important to understand in more depth the ways in which men control women.

HOW MEN CONTROL

How can you recognize controlling behavior? What are the various maneuvers that men use? How do they keep the pleaser off balance in the relationship?

I have isolated the most common patterns of controlling behavior, and as I describe them, notice the parallels to your own situation. Remember, I'm not describing types of men, but *types of behavior.* Your man may exhibit several of these behaviors or only one.

A controlling man can use many techniques, some subtle, some obvious. He can use abuse, seduction, expertise, money, empty promises, blackmail or silence to get his way so that he can feel superior. Some of these behaviors are not easy to recognize, but if you want to recover from your Me Phobia, you need to be able to clearly recognize and label controlling behavior.

Abuse

"Sometimes you make me so mad that I lose control. You'd better not push me too far because you never know what I might do to you."

The man who uses abuse to control frightens the pleaser into doing his bidding through sheer force or the threat of force. He makes his victim feel it's her fault if he abuses her. The possibility of bodily harm or extreme emotional harm is always in the back of your mind as you respond to his requests and his demands.

Most commonly, abusive behavior begins in small ways. Maybe he shoves you down on the bed or pushes you into a room where he wants to "talk to you." Except for your hurt feelings, nothing is really injured, but it becomes an unspoken threat of what might happen if he were to get really serious about keeping you in line.

The abuse escalates and you are often unclear at this stage in the relationship how much you should take. Why don't you immediately recognize the danger? Because he makes you feel like you deserve this harsh treatment. One woman whose boyfriend slapped her hard across the face reported to me that he felt very ashamed of himself afterward but told her, "I have never hit a woman in my life, but you made me so angry that I couldn't help myself." She ended up feeling responsible for driving him into such a rage.

Another woman recalled her husband telling her accusingly, "You pull the slaps out of my hand!"

Usually, by the time the abuse reaches a severe stage, you are so intimidated by what he would do if you left him that you might stay in the relationship long past the point when he is seriously hurting you.

Patty was seventeen years old and a senior in high school. She had been going with Joe since they were both twelve. She thought there was something wrong with the relationship, but she wasn't sure because it was the only one she'd ever known. One night Joe hurt her feelings by flirting in an outrageous manner with another girl in front of Patty. Patty left the party and Joe came by her home later to apologize.

This time, she wasn't sure she wanted to accept his apology. He had done this before and had apologized before. He protectively wrapped his jacket around her as they stood in front of her house, and said he was sorry and cared only for her. She didn't look at him, but mumbled something about how she had to think about this. He jerked his jacket off her and pushed her away, saying, "So, now you're not going to accept my apology. Who has been poisoning your mind against me?" She ran, crying, into the house.

This boy was being abusive, but Patty was not sure what to think. She thought maybe she *should* forgive him because, after all, he had come all the way to her house in a snowstorm, risking getting his car stuck, to apologize. She fell asleep crying with confusion. Was he abusing her or not?

Yes, Patty, he is abusing you. And if you stay in this relationship, it will get worse. Try other relationships. See that it can be different.

This happened to rock singer Tina Turner, who has recently come into the open to talk about her marriage to Ike—a relationship that was built on a pattern of abuse. When Tina finally left Ike, she was physically battered, financially broke, and psychologically intimidated. But she had seen the warning signs before she'd married him. "When he asked me to marry him, I didn't want to because I knew what my life would be like," she related in a candid interview with *Rolling Stone* magazine. "But I was afraid to say no . . . I did what Ike said. At the time, I didn't have a choice." Turner's self-esteem was so low that she couldn't recognize that she had a free will—even in the face of brutality!

Why do you stay in a relationship with a man who physically abuses you or threatens you with abuse? Frequently, the abusive man convinces you that you are somehow to blame for his behavior—like the woman who felt guilty because she had produced such a rage in her man.

If you are a pleaser, you see his abuse as disapproval of some behavior. You see being hit the same way a child experiences punishment—the direct result of wrongdoing. You are actually placing your man in the role of parent, giving him the power to define whether or not your actions are appropriate.

Taking it a step further, you might view his behavior as proof that he cares for you—that you are important enough in his life to get him upset. It may be negative attention, but it *is* attention.

If you define abuse as being cared about or being corrected for bad behavior, you are in serious danger. It usually means that you see yourself as a bad child who deserves the worst. Or you may take the abuse because when you weigh the pros and cons, you want to stay for the security or because you believe you love him.

Vickie felt trapped in this way. "He used to hit me a lot when he got angry. I remember once, after he did this, I took the kids and jumped in the car and just took off to get away from him. I was headed for the police station—I was going to turn him in. But suddenly I just stopped the car and sat there shaking and knowing I couldn't do it. I couldn't let him go—even for this. I couldn't face life without him. I couldn't stand the idea of being alone. It was so big, this thing . . . this love and need I felt."

As a pleaser, you accept the challenge: "Somehow I have failed . . . I'll try to do better in the future." But this passive response is only asking for more trouble.

Seduction

"No one can love you like I do. You're nothing without me. I'm the only one who can give you what you need."

This man not only knows how to charm *you,* but he knows exactly how to charm other women so that you are constantly kept off guard at parties and other social occasions. Sometimes you might even wonder if something is going on between him and your friends. He's so smooth, so unbearably sexy. Everyone likes him and people tell you that you're lucky to have him.

Since everyone around you approves of him, it is more difficult for you to evaluate whether or not he is a good person. Sometimes you agree with them—after all, you are charmed by him, too. At other times, you see how manipulative he is. But you work hard to be accepted by him because, if other women see him as a good catch, you think maybe something is wrong with your perception if you don't. He keeps you off balance so that you're never quite sure.

In this way, he uses other women to control you. Joan Kennedy certainly experienced that when she said of leaving Ted, "I must be crazy to be divorcing a Kennedy when every woman in America would want to change places with me."

This seductive behavior is also used by a man to control you directly. When you're angry, he knows exactly what to do and say. Flowers arrive, a special vacation is planned, there is that precious wink that promises everything will be better next time. Or he uses humor to lift you out of your anger—he can be so funny sometimes! He is a master at making excuses and making up.

Consider this scene: Paul and Mary are driving home after a party. Mary is angry because she feels Paul spent a great deal of time at the party flirting with another woman. She confronts him with this and he shrugs it off, annoyed. But Mary persists because she is feeling very hurt.

Finally, Paul says, "Okay, I know what you want," and he turns the car around and drives to a place where they used to park in high school.

Mary tries to resist but he is driving and there isn't much she can do unless she jumps out of the car—and that would be dangerous.

Paul has already started to exert his control. He parks the car and tunes into some romantic music on the radio. "Come on, honey," he urges, taking her face in his hands. "You know how much I love you. You are so beautiful, you couldn't possibly be threatened by the little bit of attention I gave Alice tonight. Are you feeling okay? Maybe you're coming down with something . . . are you starting your period? You know how sensitive you are then."

Mary starts to protest, but he stops her gently by putting his hand over her mouth. "Hush . . . hush . . . my beautiful baby. Don't be angry. It spoils your beautiful face. Just relax . . . I love you . . . I want you, only you." Mary feels her anger vanish, just as it always does when he takes her face in his hands and talks quietly about loving her. She feels her longing for him and her love for him wash over her in great waves. She can't stay angry when he's like this. She just wants to melt in his arms, and she does. Paul has won another skirmish.

Later, Mary may feel irritated when she recalls the attention Paul gave Alice at the party, and the way he blamed Mary's reaction on her period. But as her memory roams over the scene in the car, she is again touched by his tenderness and her irritation seems insignificant compared with the love she felt from him.

The seductive man makes it almost impossible for you to hang onto your anger—something you have trouble doing anyway. It never seems justified in his eyes. He reassures you that you do indeed please him; since that is your primary concern, everything else fades into the background.

Sometimes seduction comes in the form of pure, physical sex. He sees himself as sexually insatiable and believes this is proof that he is 100 percent man. Not only does he tell you that he is the only one who can satisfy you, he often reinforces your sexual appeal, saying, "Only you can make me feel this good in bed."

A man who uses sex as his primary means of seduction usually doesn't talk much. Sex is his main way of communicating. He wants to make love when he is happy . . . or when he is frustrated about work . . . or when he is angry with you . . . or when he doesn't want to talk. He uses sex like a drug; it replaces unpleasant feelings with physical ecstasy and relaxation. He is addicted to sex and the act itself controls your life.

As a pleaser in this relationship, you probably have mixed feelings about all of this sexual activity. Sometimes you feel like an object because he never seems to want to listen to you or take your needs into consideration. But other times you feel great about yourself. The fact that he thinks you're sexy and wants to make love to you makes you feel loved.

But you don't know what else it is about you that he loves, so you're afraid of not being totally available to him when he wants sex. You think that if he stops wanting you in bed, he might not want you at all. And that might not be far from the truth.

I call this type of man a "super stud." He is rarely satisfied with just one woman. His validation stems from the power he feels when he takes a woman to bed. He is usually afraid of true intimacy; the only time he experiences closeness is when he is in control. You may suspect that he is having affairs with other women or you may be so busy trying to please him that you don't even see the signs of his affairs.

I have a friend who was married for eleven years to this kind of man. It seemed like they were always climbing out of bed when anyone called, and it was a joke everyone in our circle enjoyed—even my friend and her husband.

At one point, she began getting mysterious vaginal infections. When she went to see her gynecologist he asked her about her husband's sexual patterns. She blushed and changed the subject. He tried again, asking whether either of them had sex outside of the marriage. My friend had never considered this possibility. After all, she was getting so much sex that she figured he must be getting enough, too. Her doctor knew that her husband was giving her infections that he had picked up from other women, but her denial was so strong that she couldn't hear the truth.

A sexually controlling man sees everything in the context of sex—and often he can't see you as a person at all.

"I'm a disappointment to you," she said. "I'm not the wife you hoped I would be. You are so cold to me."

"You are wrong," he replied quietly. "You were, are and always will be the wife I want, the wife I need. As for my being cold to you, I don't think you really believe that. Don't project your feelings onto me."

Francesca began to cry. She knew it was true. "Please don't give up on me," she said, watching the tears drop and spread on the tablecloth. Now why had she said that?

He wiped his lips, folded his napkin, and came around to her. He took her napkin out of her lap, dipped a corner of it into her water goblet and bathed each of her eyelids. He smoothed her heavy hair away from her face with his hands.

"Francesca, let's go to the bedroom."

—*Glass People,* by Gail Godwin
(Warner Books, 1972)

Whether your seductive mate uses words, gestures or sex, he is busy manipulating you and he is not listening to any of your concerns. He rarely focuses on how you really feel or considers why you feel that way. He meets your needs only when it is expedient. His only concern is how to coax you into feeling better so he won't have to deal with your problems. If you're angry, he'll pull a stunt like Paul did, as if to say, "I know you can't resist me when I do this."

There's a hidden threat behind this seductive behavior, too. If you don't give in, he might not be so charming anymore; you may stop pleasing him. And that is too great a risk for you to take.

Expertise

"Trust me. I know you better than you know yourself. I know what's right for you."

If an abusive man is analogous to a punishing father, a patronizing man represents a good father. He is kind and all-knowing and in the early stages of your relationship you feel wonderful because he listens to you and tries to meet your needs. He is often seen as "a good catch." You feel safe and he says he will always take care of you because he loves you. The problem here is that he is not taking care of you because he loves you. *He loves you because he can take care of you.*

A relationship with a man like this is likely to sour and his benevolence usually turns into something else. As a pleaser, you eventually try to become more of an individual because that's what you think he is encouraging you to do. (After all, isn't that what a good father does?) But he is not pleased by your demonstrations of independence; rather, he is threatened by them because they take away his position of power. The result is that he becomes critical of the very things he has been encouraging you to do. He undermines your self-confidence to satisfy his own craving for control. And you begin to see his protectiveness as a lack of respect for you.

Marilyn was a classic example of a pleasing woman in a relationship with a man who controlled her through expertise. She was only twenty when she married Jim. He was thirty-two, already successful with a thriving law practice. Marilyn adored Jim. She thought he was so smart and good. And she loved to listen to him. Sometimes, when they had friends over to dinner and Jim was expounding on some clever courtroom maneuver he had used, she found herself overwhelmed with pride and love. She felt honored that he had chosen her.

Marilyn wasn't educated like Jim. She had never been a particularly good student in high school and she had dropped out of college to marry him. She didn't ever expect to be his equal but, as a pleaser, she was concerned about being an interesting wife to him, so she made it a point to ask many questions about his work and about politics. She read the newspapers every day so she could have informed conversations with him.

Sometimes Marilyn couldn't believe she had been lucky enough to find a man like Jim. She was determined to make herself worthy of him, without him knowing it, she began to learn about local politics so she could be a more interesting conversationalist.

It took a humiliating episode to make Marilyn suspect that maybe Jim didn't *want* her to grow and change. They were at a party at Jane and Donald's house. Like all of their friends' parties, this one featured lively, intelligent conversation and sociable sparring on political issues. Marilyn really enjoyed being in the middle of such exciting conversation, and she was proud to have a few ideas of her own to air. At one point, during a heated discussion on the relative merits of two local political candidates, she spoke up—something she had rarely done in the past—and began to express a firm view. Suddenly, halfway through her statement, she looked up and saw Jim standing there, smiling with a patronizing look. "Oh, you know Marilyn," he interrupted with a laugh. "She likes to talk. Never mind that her total understanding of politics could fit into a thimble." Having brushed her aside, he then launched into an opinion of his own.

Marilyn felt her face burn with shame, but she said nothing and quickly bowed out of the conversation.

Later, Jane cornered her in the kitchen. "I can't believe you let him get away with that," she said. "It was embarrassing to watch."

"Oh," Marilyn said, shrugging, "I don't really mind. He does know more about the issues than I do. But I'm learning."

Although she denied it to her friend, Marilyn worried that she would never be able to learn enough to really please Jim. Maybe he didn't want her to learn at all. Maybe he needed to be superior and would always disapprove of her when she voiced strong opinions.

Controlling behavior of this type can sometimes be very subtle, so benevolent and caring in its expression that you have a hard time putting your finger on the problem. Even when he embarrasses you in public (as Jim did with Marilyn), there can be a tone in his voice that you might call loving. You tell yourself that he's not really putting you down, it's just that he knows best and he's protecting you from the embarrassment of being wrong. When you do feel resentment, you don't know how to articulate it—eventually, you live with a growing hurt that you can't express.

When I read the following passage in May Sarton's

book *Anger* (Norton, 1982), I felt it expressed very well the tone of the man who controls a woman by always "knowing better."

Anna had gone for a little walk around the garden, picked a small bunch of dahlias and chrysanthemums, crimson and orange, a dissonance that pleased her, when Ned came out to the porch with a tray.

"Hey," Ned said, "I call that a riot of color."

"I like it," Anna said, prickling as she always did when Ned punctured her balloons with irony.

"I would add a touch of white . . . there's that achillea somewhere."

"No," Anna said. "The whole point is that clash of primary color—not that it matters," she added. [They talked more and then she went inside to get a vase for her flowers, returning a few moments later.]

Then she saw that Ned had not been able to resist changing her bunch, had picked a spray of white anemone while she was making her mind up about the vase. Now he placed it deftly in the center of the Venetian glass with her flowers. "Perfect," he announced.

Money

"I make the money, so I have the right to make the decisions, too."

If you have no income of your own and your man gives you an allowance "for services rendered," you are probably being controlled financially. He reminds you constantly (in both direct and subtle ways) that you are completely dependent on him. He doles out the money on his own terms, as a gift ("Look how good I am to you"), in exchange for the things you have done for him, or as payment for future services. The message he communicates is one of ownership. You have to do what he says because you have no choice—if he leaves you, you'll be without resources.

Ann called in one day to my radio talk show. Her voice was shaking a little as she explained to me that she had just left her husband of twenty-eight years. I asked her why and she hesitated before answering. "I just had no love left for him . . . I didn't respect or trust him anymore."

I prodded her a little because I knew there must be more to the story. "It sounds like you feel you got a bum deal somehow," I said carefully. "What did he do that made you feel that way?"

Again, she hesitated before answering. "Well, he used to manipulate me with money," she said finally, and before I could ask for details she rushed on to add, "when we made love, he put money on the dresser."

"Oh my goodness!" I was shocked.

Her voice began to tremble as she added, "It made me hurt so bad."

"Would he make you take the money afterward?" I asked quietly.

"No . . . it would just be there."

I pressed Ann for more details. "Did you ever tell him how you felt about this?"

"I couldn't."

"Did he ever mention it?"

"No." By way of explanation she added, "He wasn't very verbal."

"Do you mind if I ask how much he gave you?"

"He gave me ten dollars," Ann said, and she seemed embarrassed by the admission. "Every time, it was the same amount . . . if it was any more, I just figured he didn't have change." Her voice cracked again. "It was just so humiliating. It ate a hole right through me."

"Why did you take it?" I asked, imagining this scene being played out for twenty-eight years.

"At first, I didn't. I'd just leave it there. And then I figured why not use it . . . he only gave me an allowance of twenty dollars every two weeks, so the extra money really helped."

Ann went on to describe the scene that finally made her decide to leave him. It was, of course, over money.

"I wanted to cash a check for fifty dollars. There were some things I needed. He started questioning me, asking me to tell him what I'd done to deserve fifty dollars. Without thinking, I began to list all the household chores I had done that day—like waxing the kitchen floor and doing the laundry, and when I was in the middle, something in me just snapped. I suddenly realized how demeaning it was."

Even if you keep the checkbook and are in charge of paying the bills, he might choose to withhold information about family finances—how much insurance you have or the value of your property, for instance. Or he may never tell you what his salary is, saying, "You have no need to know. I take care of everything, don't I?"

The man who controls you financially is often very critical of everything: the quality of your cooking, the way you keep the house, your appearance, even your sexual performance. He equates everything with money or what he terms "value." When he indicates that you may not be worth what he is spending on you, as a pleaser you feel lucky for what you get.

When you have a disagreement about something, he usually wins because he holds the trump card: "I control the purse strings around here." Money is such a powerful symbol that it is hard for you to argue with his right to set the terms of your relationship.

In thinking about what happens when men control with money, I was struck by the following passage from Ann Tyler's book *Morgan's Passing* (Berkeley Books, 1980).

"He was the jealous type, possessive, always fearing I would leave him. He never gave me any money, only charge accounts and then this teeny bit of cash for the groceries every week. For seven years I charged our food at the gourmet sections of department stores—tiny cans of ham and pure-white asparagus spears and artichoke bottoms and hearts of palm, all so I could save back some of the grocery money. I would charge a dozen skeins of yarn and then return them one by one to the Knitter's Refund counter for cash. I subscribed to every cents-off, money-back offer that came along. At the end of seven years I said, 'All right, Horace, I've saved up five thousand dollars of my own. I'm leaving.' And I left."

Think about the story of Ann earlier in this chapter. Her relationship involved an extreme of financially controlling behavior. In her husband's eyes, *every single thing she did*—including sex—had a value placed on it. His feelings of ownership were complete: he refused to pay her unless she proved her worth. While overt payment for sex is not very common, it might exist for you more subtly if you feel you owe him sex or other services because he supports you.

Empty Promises

"You drive me to distraction. If you didn't act this way, maybe I would be able to be more dependable."

The man who uses this behavior is the classic "bad boy." He might abuse alcohol or drugs, gamble, have affairs or be chronically late for every occasion. He is unreliable and you can't count on him. Often he will promise to change, but he never does. In fact, basically he believes that it's *your* problem—you expect too much.

Most likely he performs beautifully at work, where he is punctual, reliable and thoughtful. But with you he is different. The fact that he is not irresponsible when he is away from you reinforces your suspicion that you are somehow the cause of his behavior.

He is quick to blame you for the things he does that are wrong. He convinces you that there is something lacking in *you* that drives him to do these things. "You're not woman enough for me," he might say as an excuse for his affairs. Or, "I can't help drinking when you get on my case all the time."

Following is Susan's story about an evening with her boyfriend, who, she suspected, had a drinking problem.

"We were having a drink and I was pleased to see that he was nursing it slowly—lately, I'd been noticing he was drinking quite a bit. But then we got into a stupid argument about his brother and I felt he was blowing it out of proportion. It really wasn't that big a deal. Suddenly, he jumped to his feet in a rage and stormed into the kitchen. He came back with a bottle of bourbon and gave me a very nasty look. 'You are such a bitch sometimes,' he said in the meanest voice. And then he took the top off the bottle and drank a third of it in one gulp. I was horrified. I'd never seen anything like this. He kind of staggered back into his chair and gave me this smug look like, 'see what happens when you get on my nerves.'

"Later," Susan said, "when he sobered up, he apologized and promised that he would never behave that way again. But of course he did."

Often, this is the way it is in relationships between women who accept the blame and men who are irresponsible. Since you feel you are the cause for his behavior—and, most likely, he does too—you concentrate your energies on trying to please him so he won't be "forced" to break his promises or resume his bad habits. And that's how he controls you so that you never cause a fuss, make him feel guilty or threaten to leave him.

Eventually, broken promises become the focal point of your relationship. You allow them because you are certain you can turn the tide with your love. For some women, this goes on for years.

After his last affair with his secretary, John promised Sarah that he would change. They went to a marriage counselor and he even bought her a new wedding band to symbolize the beginning of a new life together. She was thrilled and trusted him completely even though he had been having one affair after another since the beginning of their six-year marriage.

In this atmosphere of total trust, John began another liaison, this time with the marriage counselor they were seeing. Although it was going on right under her nose, Sarah never noticed a thing.

Soon John and the counselor began seeing each other for lunch on a regular basis and that's how Sarah found out the ugly truth.

She was particularly embarrassed because some of her friends were eating at the same restaurant and brought her the news. She struggled to cover for him and then confronted him that evening with her rage and despair.

He blamed her; he said she deserved it. "Anyone so dumb that she can't see something that is going on before her very eyes deserves to be fooled." When that didn't work and she continued to rage at him, he tried to laugh it off and said it was all her imagination. That didn't work either.

He ended the conversation by saying that she should try to be more like the counselor, then maybe their marriage would work.

Sarah thought this over and since she had admired

the counselor very much, she decided that he might be right. They changed therapists and to this day they are still married . . . and he is still having affairs.

Another aspect of irresponsible behavior is that it often brings out the "punishing mother" in you. Once you are entrenched in that pattern, it becomes a vicious cycle. He will rebel against what he imagines to be your control and then act up even more, causing you to try harder to get him to shape up. That gives him more to rebel against, as well as a rationalization for his actions.

If your man is a chronic breaker of promises who exhibits this "bad boy" behavior, you are probably embarrassed by him and you try to keep it a secret from everyone, even your closest friends. You spend a lot of energy trying to project a "perfect relationship." You are not only trying to please him, you are also trying to look good to others. The importance you place on looking good is something he knows about. He can get back at you because he knows how miserable you become when he behaves badly.

You try to please him so he will be good so you can look good.

When that doesn't work and he wins the struggle, you get angry . . . and this is followed by the withholding or punishing behavior that only encourages him to continue.

You feel responsible for him, guilty when he messes up and worried about him when he is at his worst, but he gives you the illusion of being the superior one, the one in control. That alone can keep you coming back for more broken promises.

Emotional Blackmail

"Watch yourself . . . or you'll be sorry."

While the man who acts bad keeps you in check by blaming you, the man who blackmails makes it clear that he will tarnish your "good girl" image if you don't behave. In one sense, he makes you just as bad as he is—at least in his mind—thereby protecting himself from your criticism. He also knows how important it is that you look good to the outside world and he holds this as a threat over your head. He may even lead you into some "bad behavior" and then use the threat of disclosure to control you.

Marty, a woman I counseled several years ago, had a story like this. She and her husband had been to Mexico and when they were ready to return to the United States, he said casually, "I want you to do something for me." She said, "Of course," and he pulled out a plastic bag of cocaine.

"He wanted me to help him get it over the border," she told me, her voice shaking from the memory. "He asked me to hide it in a Kotex and wear the Kotex across. I was very upset by the request . . . but I did it. And he never let me live it down that I was a 'drug smuggler.' "

By emphasizing something that you have done, this man also minimizes your right to correct any of his behavior. "If you have done that, I don't think you have the right to tell me what is right or wrong," he says. He plays on your need for fairness and uses this maneuver to sidestep your criticism.

Emotional blackmail can be about anything. Perhaps he knows that you cheated on an important examination in college. Maybe you were once caught shoplifting. Or he knows that you took drugs when you were younger. Whatever your secret is, his hold on you lies in his threat of exposure and your need to keep a lid on the information. One woman I counseled was afraid to leave her husband because he threatened to take her to court and get custody of the children; she'd had a problem with tranquilizers ten years earlier. Even though it was a thing of the past (in fact, it was before her children were born), she was afraid that he would succeed in winning if her secret were revealed.

Usually he takes something he already knows about you and blows it out of proportion, but sometimes he may search for a flaw so he can use it as a pawn. I once knew a man who hired a detective to follow his wife; it took years (and much money) to catch her doing something "wrong." He discovered her going to school behind his back—spending *his* money without permission. For that, he called her a thief and a liar. She had to agree with him and from then on he "had" her and often referred to that "scandalous time." She is still suffering for the embarrassment she caused him.

The Silent Treatment

"I know you can't stand it when I turn you off and pretend like you don't exist. You'll do anything to get me talking again."

The woman who aims to please is putty in the hands of a man who uses the silent treatment to get what he wants. He uses one of the most frightening controlling maneuvers: when he turns off verbally and emotionally, he withholds the clues that you depend on, the clues you need to decide how to react in a given situation. The vacuum he creates to punish you when he is displeased with you totally undermines your self-confidence. You would prefer almost any other response—put-downs, seduction, accusations, even physical abuse—at least then you can react to something. The emptiness of his indifference makes you feel crazy.

Just as you would prefer any response from him other than silence, you will do almost anything to get him to talk to you again—cry, threaten, even lash out with violence to change the situation. You are, of course, ripe for manipulation. He has only to say something like, "Just admit you are wrong and it'll be okay," or "Promise me you will quit that silly job of yours and we can stop this ridiculous game." Most often, his suggestions are too tempting to resist and the alternative too painful to contemplate. How could you manage if this silent treatment went on much longer?

You are humiliated if he starts the silent treatment in public. You will do almost anything to placate him so you won't be embarrassed—and this gives him considerable control over you. The silent treatment (which is a bit like a quiet temper tantrum, when you think about it) can go on for days, weeks, months . . . even years.

A woman who called my radio program told me about an extreme example of the silent treatment.

"I found some credit-card receipts that showed my husband had bought flowers for someone two thousand miles away—I think maybe he's having an affair with someone while he's on business trips. But I'm too scared to ask him about it."

"Why?" I asked. "Are you afraid he'll get angry?"

"It's not just that," she said. "Eight years ago there was an incident. We went to a party and he flirted with this other woman all evening, leaving me alone at a table. On our way home, I mentioned I was a little jealous—I didn't even make a big thing of it. But he punished me with silence for eight months—no touching, no sex, no talking. It was a nightmare. Finally, one day he bought me a big present and expected everything to go back to normal. It took me five years to get over it. And I'm scared about what he'll do this time."

One woman in my neighborhood confided in me that she had lived with a silent husband for three years before she finally left him. It all started over a disagreement about her cat.

She had gotten Scruffy long before she'd met and married her husband. The animal had never given them much trouble, but eventually age began to take its toll and Scruffy had problems with incontinence. She wanted to get him medical treatment. Her husband wanted to put him to sleep. It became a terrible struggle and he stopped talking to her.

Neither of them realized that the husband's negative feelings about the cat came from the fact that the animal reminded him of his wife's life before him, when she had dated extensively. This became clear only several years after the divorce.

At first, the silence didn't bother her too much because she felt so strongly about her cat. She took Scruffy to a vet and he improved considerably—but the same thing didn't happen with her husband's mood. She tried to talk to him. When that didn't work, she pleaded with him. Finally, after several months, she began having crying jags.

Then she got busy at her job and decided to wait him out. This acceptance of the situation lasted almost two years, he completely silent and she, patient and humble. Then she got depressed and one night, after several glasses of wine, took an overdose of pills. He took her to the hospital but never uttered a word to her. That was it! After regaining consciousness, she promised herself that if she survived, she would get a divorce. She had finally realized how angry she was.

As we talked in my living room, years after this terrible time in her life, she admitted that she had let him get away with using the silent treatment many times before this incident. She had given up her garden because he liked store-bought vegetables better than those she grew. She had stopped going to her Great Books Club at the local library because he wanted her home every night. For each of these offenses, he had become silent for a day or two and she had relented rather than live with what she called "a ghost of a man."

Her motto had been: "Anything to keep the marriage peaceful ... anything to please him ... anything not to be left."

If the silent treatment works once, this kind of man will use it again and again, like the other maneuvers he uses to get his way. And the stakes will become higher.

HOW THESE TACTICS KEEP YOU IN LINE

Now you understand the specific tactics of the controlling man, and which ones are relevant in your relationship. But you still may be unclear about why these controlling maneuvers work so well, keeping you a pleaser.

Start from the premise that you are insecure about the relationship. You feel you are nothing if you can't make him happy. Furthermore, you have given him power over you—if he praises you, you're good; if he criticizes you, you're bad. He uses the influence on you that you have permitted him.

He threatens you with your most basic fears: abandonment, a sense of complete failure, feelings of no personal worth. Each controlling tactic undermines your confidence in a slightly different way. Each holds a different hammer over your head:

— Abuse/blackmail: The threat is physical pain and punishment. The real fear is death.
— Seduction: The threat is rejection for another woman. The real fear is abandonment.
— Money: The threat is taking away the most basic needs. The real fear is poverty.
— Silence: The threat is loneliness, having no one to talk to. The real fear is isolation.

— Empty promises: The threat is more trouble. The real fear is that you will have no one to trust or depend on.
— Expertise: The threat is being unable to manage. The real fear is failure.

Scratch the surface of every pleaser and you'll find the terror of becoming a "bag woman." Why? Because you know how hazardous your position as a pleaser is. It's a lot like building a castle on quicksand . . . the castle is bound to sink eventually and you know it. He cannot give you security and self-esteem. That must come from within. But as long as you live out the fantasy that it can work for you, his controlling maneuvers will have tremendous power.

They also have power because of the rewards they seem to hold for you if you succeed in making him happy. He leads you to believe that pleasing him can bring you love, security, acceptance, and confidence. Each controlling behavior pattern holds out a different carrot:

— Abuse/blackmail: The carrot is an end to fear and intimidation.
— Seduction: The carrot is romance and love.
— Money: The carrot is financial security.
— Silence: The carrot is connectedness; never being lonely.
— Empty promises: The carrot is a responsible, caring man.
— Expertise: The carrot is that you will be cared for and have security.

The threats and rewards of each controlling tactic should now be clearer. Recognizing what is happening and being able to label what you see is a great step forward. You are beginning to develop the awareness that will eventually give you the power to overcome Me Phobia.

The second part of step three in your recovery is coming up in the next chapter—a look at your responses to the controlling tactics I have described here, and why they are bound to fail.

4

YOUR RESPONSE
TO HIS CONTROL

Can you see now why the controlling tactics of your man make you feel so trapped? On the one hand, he holds out the chance for you to win those ultimate rewards, love, happiness, security, and success. You can have them all . . . if only you please him.

On the other hand, there's the constant shadow of a threat: "Displease me and I'll leave you . . . you'll be alone, a failure."

According to his dictate, it's up to you. If it doesn't work out, it's your fault.

No wonder you feel guarded and defensive! Who wouldn't faced with such a scenario? And it's easy to see how you can fall into the trap of living to please him. He is the actor, you the reactor. He takes the offensive, you the defensive . . . two very frightened people, he in the "one-up" and you in the "one-down" position, digging in your heels with no real chance for intimacy. Both of you protecting your own flanks.

Indeed, you're not just floating aimlessly in your relationship with the controlling man. You're very busy protecting yourself, and this protection takes many forms, just as the behavior of the controlling man takes many forms.

Chances are, you will see yourself reflected in one or more of the reactive behaviors described in this chapter. Let me note here that I am not trying to put you down when I describe these behaviors . . . only hoping to help you begin to see the vicious cycle of control and counter-control that marks a relationship between a controlling man and a pleasing woman.

COUNTER-CONTROL

You may find it difficult to admit that you, too, are a controlling person in your relationship. As we continue with step three, you will begin to realize how you use *counter-*controlling maneuvers to handle his behavior and keep yourself "alive." The control you struggle to exert is defensive—directly related to him. You may choose escape—running away from the situation as much as possible. Or you may sneak around and get what you want and need behind his back—like the woman who hid her purchases in the back of the closet because she didn't want her husband to know about them. Maybe you burst into tears or otherwise strive to win his sympathy (and the display of his comfort). Or you fight back, play it tough. Maybe none of these responses reflects your behavior and you are the ultimate pleaser, stuck in your role of being the "little girl" to his "big man."

You might protest, "but that's just the way I am." I would suggest that if you are a pleasing woman in a relationship with a controlling man, none of these responses reflects the way you really are. Rather, you are reacting to your man. Remember that you have not chosen these maneuvers consciously—they are unconscious knee-jerk reactions to the perception of danger. As you read this chapter, think about which style (or styles) best describes you. And think also about why you have chosen your particular method. (Was it, for example, the way your mother handled your father?)

Later in this chapter, we'll talk about why your counter-controlling tactics fail to work—and, in fact, make you feel worse about yourself, reinforcing your Me Phobia.

THE COUNTER-CONTROLLING MANEUVERS

Escape From Reality

On the surface, you may appear to cater to your man on just about every issue. You seem to be cooperative and even happy in your relationship. But in reality, you are involved in a deal, not a relationship—and your man might not even be aware of the terms.

While you are pretending to cater to him, there is a secret, separate aspect to your life.

Katherine had been playing this game in her marriage for ten years when she came to see me. She had a small side business designing children's clothing— a business her husband knew nothing about. Or, to be accurate, he knew that she did some sewing, but he believed it was just a hobby, something to fill her time.

The reason Katherine came to see me was that her business had become so successful that it had attracted media attention, bringing her secret out into the open. When her husband found out what was really going on, he flew into a rage. He accused her of deceiving him (which she had been) and demanded to know where the money had gone. Somehow he had reached the conclusion that she was using the money to finance affairs with other men. When he saw what little control he really had over her, he began to imagine that there were many other secrets Katherine might be hiding from him.

Katherine was devastated and hurt by her husband's reaction. Her escape maneuver had worked for so long, so successfully, that she was terrified now of facing him. She could no longer escape into the world of her business and be free and safe from his opinions and his threats of anger. Her business had been her haven. Now that was over.

At some deep, nagging level, Katherine realized that the way she had been compartmentalizing her life had not been healthy. She knew that she had looked forward to those few hours a day when she could be true to herself, and the rest of the time she had been living a lie. She also noticed that lately she had become more angry with her husband for making her feel that she had to live that way.

When I suggested to Katherine that she was not

being *forced* to live like this, she seemed startled. I explained that I thought she had become so Me Phobic that she couldn't risk bringing more of her true self into her daily life. She had comfortably slotted two hours a day when she could focus on her own needs—and she was actually afraid of what would happen if she expanded that time. By compartmentalizing, Katherine was hiding from herself. She was afraid that if she really examined her feelings, she might find that she wanted more involvement with her business, which would surely clash with what her husband wanted of her.

I asked Katherine to think about the possibility that her husband might be afraid of losing her if he couldn't control her. She had never entertained that idea, having put all her energies into her own fear of being left if she didn't please him. But the idea made her feel stronger, and she gave up her original idea of closing her business. If he had fears, too, maybe she could help him overcome them by being more herself in the marriage. It was a courageous move on Katherine's part.

This story has a happy ending. Katherine and her husband did stay together, she eventually opened a children's clothing store . . . and her husband became her greatest fan. Today Katherine feels more confident about herself, and her husband feels better about himself, too, now that he realizes that she loves him for who he is, not for his financial support.

Perhaps you are escaping in some way or another from your relationship. You might not have a secret career like Katherine did, but you may hide purchases from your husband or go out with friends when you tell him you are doing something else. One

woman I met in Minneapolis while I was doing a
television show on the subject of secrets reported
that she bought groceries at one store, but told her
husband she was shopping at another—the one he
recommended.

Maybe you escape into your career and have become a workaholic, or perhaps you are totally im-
mersed in your children or your volunteer work.
Some women use alcohol, drugs, or eating to escape.
A growing number of women are having outside affairs as a way of emotionally separating themselves
from controlling men. I know one woman who is totally wrapped up in exercise and perfecting her body,
and another who has escaped by throwing herself
into the activities of a group that believes in channel-
ing—listening to voices from the past.

Whether you escape through spirituality, career,
children or alcohol, it never works in the long run.
You are merely protecting yourself from him, and
forfeiting any possibility of true intimacy in your relationship. Moreover, you can never really find yourself
or be content if you use other activities to hide from
the way you really feel.

Conning Him

If you use this maneuver, you know how to get what
you want or protect yourself while still playing the
pleaser. You are probably very bright and very witty.
You know how to duck and weave, avoiding his
punches like a seasoned boxer. You may use sex,
humor and smart-talking to ingratiate yourself and
manipulate him.

Maybe you're not even aware of how much time you spend trying to control his responses and how much of yourself you are losing in the process. After all, you appear to be so self-confident!

One woman described to me how she used humor to "jolly my husband out of his anger. Rick was very short-tempered and I used to spend a lot of time figuring out how to avoid a blowup. I knew if I could get him laughing at something, it would probably be okay."

Another woman I know had deep fears about her husband's behavior, but she covered them up by being clever and successful. Marcia was a smart talker; she had a bright answer to everything. She gave the appearance of being in perfect control of her life. Ironically, this only made her husband's behavior worse since he was threatened by her show of strength.

Maybe it's hard for you to see yourself in this role, precisely because you *do* appear to be so strong and self-confident. That's one of the problems with this form of behavior. You have convinced yourself that you are in control of the relationship, losing sight of how frightened you once felt by his controlling maneuvers—until you discovered this way around the problem.

Why not face it—*you are still being controlled by him*. Aren't you exhausted sometimes by the effort (or challenge) of never being able to really relax when he is around? Aren't you tired of having to figure out how to help him feel better about himself so he won't be too hard on you? Aren't you sick of having to phrase any criticism, no matter how small, in the most diplomatic of terms? You may have fooled the outside world into thinking you have everything under control . . . but don't fool yourself.

Feeling Down and Out

This kind of behavior is not unlike what a rat does in an experimental situation. The rat is not given any consistent reward system—for example, he may be randomly shocked. At first, he panics and runs around the cage trying everything he can to avoid the painful stimulation. After the panic, he stops his frantic behavior but still exhibits signs of severe anxiety or stress (defecating, urinating, raised pulse and respiration). Finally, though, he seems to give up and become depressed. Researchers call this state "learned helplessness."

This is a paradigm for the state you may fall into when you feel that there is no way to win. Your pleasing behavior hasn't worked, the emotional pain has grown acute, and you see no way out. You pass through the frantic phase, the anxious phase and finally adopt a defeated position, hoping against hope that your man will see your despair and offer his sympathy. You may cry a lot or you may be past the point of crying, numbed by your pain. In any case, you are depressed and you have a severe case of Me Phobia. You can no longer focus on yourself or meet your own needs; you feel hopeless about anything being of help. You have no energy left to try changing your relationship.

Susan is so depressed that she has trouble getting

out of bed, and many days she doesn't even bother dressing. For five years, she has been engaged in a struggle with her live-in boyfriend to get a commitment for marriage. She is anxious to tie the knot because she is thirty-five years old and wants children, but he keeps putting her off. Susan thinks she loves Kevin but sometimes, when she realizes how much she has changed since she met him, she wonders if he is really good for her. She used to be healthy, slim, and full of energy. Now she is overweight, allergic to almost everything, and very tired. Her doctor can't understand what is happening but she suspects the truth.

Susan knows that she needs Kevin so badly that she has given up everything to make the relationship work—even if it works only on his terms. He continues to evade her pressure to marry, and yet he makes it seem like it's right around the corner. She has grown too tired to fight him, although she knows she should make him move out. And she is too ashamed of herself to try to find another man. So she lets things slide . . . and she cries.

Susan cries every day. She feels that Kevin has won and she is now powerless. She doesn't plan to ask him about marriage anymore. *Maybe this is better than nothing. Maybe this is all she will ever get. Maybe this is all she deserves.*

When you're this depressed, negativity colors your thinking. You get used to seeing yourself in a disparaging light. You feel that your situation is without hope and the world is overwhelming and hostile. The more these thoughts cloud your vision, the deeper your despair becomes. I have never met a woman who has been able to get out of this trap without professional help.

Expressing Anger

On the surface, it may seem that you have a clear sense of yourself and have no trouble expressing anger. You frequently put your man down. You nag him. Sometimes you explode in a rage. Maybe your friends even view you as the powerhouse of the relationship—they see you as being in control of him. And in this way, you control the public perception of your relationship.

Your man rarely stands up to you in public or counters your anger with his own. He might laugh it off with a comment about your "gestapo tactics" or kid you, saying, "You're so cute when you're angry." Maybe he ignores your anger, passively letting it slide by. That is usually the clue to the underlying fact of the matter, which is that you are doing this only *with his permission.* You can antagonize him, but you are allowed only to go so far . . . and you both know it.

Your angry behavior makes you a prime candidate for Me Phobia because the energy of your rebellion keeps you armed and on guard, with very little time to focus on yourself.

You are not unlike the small child who is confronted on the street by a big scary dog. As they stare at each other, the child may handle her fear by "barking" at the dog in a loud and threatening voice. In this way, she identifies with the aggressor by acting like the object that is so terrifying. Among children, this is a common way to handle fear.

In her book, *The Myth of Female Masochism* (Dutton, 1985), Paula J. Caplan, Ph.D., discusses the defensive behavior that is often at the root of women's aggression.

> "For women whose husbands periodically humiliate or abuse them, emotionally or physically, the waiting period before the next assault can arouse intense anxiety. These women may find that the only way to stop the anxiety is to precipitate the assault as soon as possible, to get it over with for the time being. Some battered wives say that the only aspect of their lives over which they have control is the *timing* of the beatings they receive."

Even while you're asserting yourself and making a point of taking a firm stand, often you're deliberately taking an adversary position to your controlling man. You're reacting to him.

Joanne called me on the radio because she and her husband, Frederick, were fighting all the time. "We're completely different individuals," she said. "We can't get along because we always want to go in opposite directions. We have different ideas about style and completely opposite views of what is right and wrong." Joanne was convinced that they should divorce.

Then I asked her what kind of a man she would want. She seemed confused, and puzzled over the question a moment before answering. "I don't know," she said finally. "I've been so busy struggling to have some influence in my marriage that I guess I lost track of what I want. For example, Frederick always plans vacations where we just relax and sit in the sun, and I always say I'd rather do something different. The truth is, if I could plan them, I'd probably choose to do the same thing. I guess I resent his 'take charge' attitude."

Joanne couldn't see that she had lost herself in her marriage years ago and that she was now using her fights with Frederick as reassurance that she was still a person, rather than as a true expression of her wants and needs.

Sometimes anger isn't your primary way of reacting to your man's behavior, but something happens to make you explode. A woman called my radio show to tell me about how critical her husband was of her. She actually sounded proud of the way she handled his anger in an agreeable way. "He can get mean, but I love him and I try to calm things down," she explained.

She was calling me not because she found this arrangement intolerable, but because she had recently "lost control," as she put it, and was worried about how to get back into his good graces.

He had been criticizing her because she had forgotten something at the supermarket, and, tired of his constant nagging, she just exploded and told him to get off her back. He reacted by flying into a tremendous rage (he had been drinking at the time) and threatening some harm toward her twenty-one-year-old daughter, his stepdaughter. The girl left the house and hid in the garage.

After that, the caller told me, she tried to calm him

down, not knowing how to handle her own feelings of anger or his reaction to them. After years of deferring to him, she had built up so much frustration that she didn't know how to handle the rage that surged out.

When you display rightful anger, your controlling man might accuse you of being a "ball buster" or blame you for his own anger. And you find that aggressive behavior only makes the situation worse, because it is not pleasing to him.

Keeping the Peace

If you are the ultimate pleaser, you're going to want to keep the peace at any price and agree to everything your man proposes. And if you're very dependent on him financially, you're more likely to do this.

Perhaps you've convinced yourself that this is the way it's supposed to be. You love your man and live totally for and through him. In fact, you don't keep *anything* for yourself—even the privacy of your own thoughts and feelings. Chances are, you don't even know how to describe the ways you feel.

The most famous example of this kind of behavior comes from eighteenth-century literature in Henrik Ibsen's portrait of Nora in the play *A Doll's House.*

(Nora, speaking to her husband near the end of the play)

NORA: When I lived at home with Papa, he told me all his opinions, so I had the same ones too; or if they were different I hid them, since he wouldn't have cared for that. He used to call me his doll-child, and he played with me the way I played with my dolls. Then I came into your house—

HELMER: How can you speak of our marriage like that?

NORA: [*unperturbed*] I mean, then I went from Papa's hands into yours. You arranged everything to your own taste, and so I got the same taste as you—or I pretended to; I can't remember . . . I guess a little of both, first one, then the other. Now when I look back, it seems as if I'd lived here like a beggar—just from hand to mouth. I've lived by doing tricks for you, Torvald. But that's the way you wanted it . . . And you've always been so kind to me. But our home's been nothing but a playpen. I've been your doll-wife here, just as at home I was Papa's doll-child. And in turn the children have been my dolls . . .

This play is a spectacularly accurate portrait of a relationship between a man who uses protection or expertise to control his wife and a woman who acts submissively as a tactic of counter-control. The only missing piece in the play is that Nora never acknowledges that she is as responsible as he is for the inequality in their marriage. But the times were different then, and she was playing out the role that society expected of women. Today, as the 1980s draw to a close, things have changed dramatically. The image of the perfect wife is no longer that of a woman who is completely deferential to her husband.

The change in society's definition of what a woman should be to a man poses a problem for the woman who is the ultimate pleaser. The role does not play as easily as it did in Nora's time. There is tremendous pressure for women not to be subservient.

If you tend to submit to your man in everything, no doubt you struggle somewhat with this problem. Everything you read and see on television negates the role you have chosen. Your friends want to know about *you*. At parties people ask you what you do and they want to hear something that conveys your individuality. You struggle hard to repress the natural pressure from inside to grow and become independent. And you're afraid to let your real feelings show through because you risk losing the hold you have on your man.

If you live with a controlling man, you have probably used more than one of these responses to handle his behavior. You may have on occasion—or regularly—used the gamut of reactions, as Anna was accused of doing in this excerpt from May Sarton's novel *Anger* (Norton, 1982):

Anna turned over for the tenth time and tried to force herself to relax, but if she managed to let the tension go from her arm, it was there in her leg, then in her neck. She looked at her watch. It was only two A.M. And suddenly she was furious with that inert sleeping man who understood nothing and gave nothing. Unable to contain so much fury, she took him by the throat and shook him awake. [Then he accused her of being mad and of upsetting the dog who always slept at the bottom of their bed. She replied:]

"Why can't you be more loving? Why? Why?"

"Don't ask me to do what I can't do," Ned said coldly.

"But why can't you?"

This time Ned was angry enough himself to answer, "Because I don't feel like it."

Tears poured down Anna's cheeks.

"Now we have to have the whole gamut from a violent physical attack to hysterical weeping, I suppose," [*Ned responded*].

This brings up the interesting question of whether or not your controlling man sees your reactions to his behavior as attempts to control *him*. Is he or is he not aware of your efforts to handle him? And does he see them as conscious maneuvers or spontaneous reactions? The more hostile (and thus more frightened) controlling man will probably see your reactions as efforts to control him and use that as a rationale for escalating his controlling tactics, as Ned did in the above scene.

Julie, a woman who came to see me about her faltering marriage, told me that her husband had been withdrawing from her. "I know something's wrong, but when I try to ask him about it, he gets hostile. He says things like, 'Just leave me alone,' and 'Stop trying to run my life.' I'm not trying to run his life . . . I just want us to be happy. But it's reached the point where I'm afraid to even suggest any plans because I'm afraid he'll say I'm trying to control him."

Julie was frightened by her husband's reaction and she vehemently denied any effort to control him. But her great guilt and fear increased her protective mechanisms and further undermined her already low self-esteem.

DOES YOUR COUNTER-CONTROL WORK?

By now, you have probably identified the profile that best describes the way you characteristically handle your controlling man. It is unlikely that you have ever stopped to think about whether or not your counter-control tactics work to make your relationship better. Sadly, your focus has probably been on how these tactics protect you from getting hurt.

Now, give it some thought:

— Does your reaction to him—the counter-controlling behavior you use—make your relationship seem better?
— Does it protect you and make you feel safer in the relationship?
— Does it make him less controlling?
— Does it bring greater intimacy to your relationship?

Let's take the last question first. Certainly none of the tactics described in this chapter work to make your relationship more intimate. Intimacy exists in a relationship when both people can meet their own needs and those of their partner in a reciprocal way. If you lose yourself in reacting to your controlling man (rather than *relating* to him), you also lose the possibility of working toward the kind of relationship I know you so desperately want. You have made it impossible to meet your own needs and difficult for your partner to do the same, as we discussed in the first chapter.

Now, ask yourself whether your counter-controlling tactics have changed your man's behavior in a positive direction. The answer is probably a resounding *no!* Since the basic motivation of your tactics is to please him and prevent rejection, you are just digging a deeper hole in your Me Phobia. By making yourself a doormat, you encourage him to become even more controlling.

These tactics also tend to make him lose respect for you—so how can you really protect yourself from rejection? Time and time again, I have seen the most loving, most cooperative, most subservient woman being left by her man for a more exciting rival. Your tactics do not buy you the security you want. Nor do they prepare you to function as an independent human being if the relationship ends.

Ultimately, the reason these tactics don't work is that you are not relating honestly to your man. They are all based on presenting a front or an image. You fight against letting the real you shine through.

If you are like most women, you try to cover up the situation as far as the rest of the world is concerned. You may minimize the problem . . . "How he treats me is not a big deal. Basically, we have a good relationship." Or you may normalize things . . . "Isn't it terrible, but I guess it's just the cross we women have to bear." Or you may make excuses for him . . . "Don't mind him, he's been working hard lately." You may even blame yourself for his behavior . . . "I haven't been myself these days. Usually, he's not this unreasonable." You might blame the children, telling them, "Daddy wouldn't stay out so late if you kids would behave." Or you might say of another adult, "That friend of his is a terrible influence. I wish he would leave town so things would get back to normal."

All of the justifications make it harder to see the

truth about your real situation. Sometimes your denial is so strong that you begin to believe your own excuses. At other times, you may reserve the truth for a special person, a close confidant who knows the real truth. This person might be a friend, your mother, or a prospective lover, and your relationship with the confidant amounts to a kind of emotional infidelity to your man. If your friends or relatives know more about you than your man does, think about what this means—and what your role is in allowing it to happen. When he notices that you confide in others, he may feel rejected, and his increased fear of losing you makes him crank up his controlling maneuvers even more.

I'm not trying to make you feel bad about yourself when I tell you these things. I'm only trying to show you that any behavior that falls short of honest inward-looking only makes your situation worse and increases your Me Phobia. I want you to be able to see that the tactics you use to try to save your relationship are often responsible for ending it altogether.

In the next chapter I'll take it a step further and show you how you are not personally to blame for the way you behave in relationships with men. As a woman, you have received plenty of conditioning that makes you susceptible to controlling men. Your understanding of these conditioning factors will give you a clearer sense of how you came to lose track of your true self in your desire to please your man.

5

CONDITIONED TO PLEASE

There has been a lot written in recent years about how women are "socialized" differently than men. In this chapter, you'll see how your conditioning has played an important role in the development of your pleasing behavior.

This awareness is step four in your recovery from Me Phobia. You will begin to understand that your behavior today did not spring from a vacuum; rather, it was cultivated by a long series of socialization factors.

I know that it's easy for women to read books like this one and end up feeling guilty about how they've allowed themselves to be controlled by their men. I hope this chapter will help you go a little easier on yourself. You'll begin to see that, in large part, your role as a pleaser did not develop through conscious choice. The process has had much more to do with society's influence on you throughout your life . . . and even before you were born.

BEFORE YOU WERE BORN

There was one important factor already at work before you were born that would clearly affect the way you were to feel about yourself as a female . . . and would start you on the road to becoming a pleaser: *Your parents would probably have preferred a boy.*

Before you object and say, "Maybe in other families, but not in mine," or "That's so old-fashioned," let me run a few statistics by you that Letty Cottin Pogrebin made famous in her book, *Growing Up Free* (McGraw Hill, 1980).

— For an only child, over ninety percent of the men and two-thirds of the women prefer a son.
— For a first-born, eighty percent want a son—only four percent of the men and ten percent of the women want a daughter.
— For a three-child family, most prefer two boys and one girl, rather than two girls and one boy.

This preference for boys has to make its mark, no matter how subtly it is communicated. I think it goes a long way toward explaining why young girls begin their pattern of pleasing in order to win the love and acknowledgment of their parents—they feel there is something defective about themselves, even though they don't know what it is, and they set about to capture the elusive love that seems to be withheld.

Even if you were fortunate enough to be a wanted baby girl, the socialization process that begins at birth is bound to have had an affect on you.

It's surprising to realize how little has changed about the way children are raised. Strong stereotypes still exist: Girls are raised to be more passive than active, more weak than strong. And boys, while they may be now willing to play with dolls, often use those dolls, according to Warren Farrell, Ph.D., in *Why Men Are the Way They Are,* only to expand the repertoire by which they can either perform or kill.

Recently I was observing the children of friends of mine. Jan and Bob have a six-year-old daughter, Emily, and a four-year-old son, Peter. They are a very modern family in every way; both Bob and Jan consider themselves to be "liberated" in the way they raise their children.

But their conversation often contains comments like, "Peter is all boy . . . he's such a tough little guy." And, "Emily, you're so sweet the way you help Mommy."

Jan and Bob are not the only ones who make these remarks about their children—all of us do. It's almost an automatic reaction.

Peter carries his little body with supreme self-confidence. He shirks hugs and kisses and prefers to play alone. He is noisy, creative, and outspoken about what he wants.

Emily is a contrast to her brother. When guests are visiting, she always finds a way into their laps. She compliments them profusely about their looks and repeatedly asks if she can serve them food and drinks. Everyone reinforces Emily's pleasing behavior by commenting on what a lovely and polite little girl she is. Privately, her mother worries.

"Emily seems so needy," she remarked to me one day. "If I get angry or criticize her, she'll go off by herself and cry. She gets very upset if she thinks someone doesn't like her, and she's always in turmoil over her friends. If she wants to sit in Bob's lap and he says no because he's busy with something, she'll run to her room in tears. I don't know what to do about it."

The conditioning to please that Emily has already received by the age of six has shaped her basic worldview; it will be hard to change. And Jan and Bob aren't even aware that they support this behavior by limiting their praise of Emily to the times she behaves in a "feminine" manner.

They are not alone in this. It's well-known that parents (even when they are well-meaning) speak differently to girls than they do to boys. They handle boys in a rougher manner. They react differently to their behavior. For example, Jan will criticize Emily when she plays outside and gets her clothes dirty, but this is expected of Peter. She fondly refers to him as "my little mud ball."

Boys are encouraged to spend more time playing outside the house, while girls are rewarded for staying in—no wonder boys are more adventuresome! Little boys are dressed more often in blues and other bright colors, which are considered by neurologists to be more stimulating than the soft pastels often reserved for girls.

The list is endless. And while these may seem to be small distinctions that have little consequence, they add up to a total picture of differences.

Researchers who have found that girls have a preference for attachment over independence think that
the major consequence of this socializing factor is a
great fear of separation. Whenever I get ready to
leave Jan and Bob's house after a visit, Emily throws
her arms around my neck and demands to know exactly when I'll be coming back. Jan once said that
every time I leave, Emily is afraid she'll never see me
again.

"That's ridiculous," I protested. "She sees me every
couple of months."

"I know," said her mother. "But she's always convinced that the people she loves will disappear."

In her book *In a Different Voice—Psychological
Theory and Women's Development* (Harvard Uni-
versity Press, 1982), Carol Gilligan describes the attitudes of two eleven-year-old children, Jake and Amy.
She shows how Jake's concerns are more inner-
focused, while Amy always makes decisions in the
framework of her entire circle of friends. Notes
Gilligan:

Describing himself as distinct by locating his
particular position in the world, Jake sets himself
apart from that world by his abilities, his beliefs
and his height. Although Amy also enumerates her
likes, her wants and her beliefs, she locates herself
in relation to the world, describing herself through
actions that bring her into connection with others,
elaborating ties through her ability to provide help.

You might ask: Do these differences really add up
to putting females at a disadvantage? Aren't social
skills important to the development of an individual?

Indeed they are. But the tendency to be outer-focused and concerned with the needs of others in preference to your own is exactly the kind of pleasing behavior that gets you into trouble later on. When you define yourself only in terms of how well you are able to meet others' needs, you never find out who *you* really are.

It's not surprising that many young girls become very anxious about being alone, and prefer attachment to separation. From early on, they are raised to be afraid of the outside world—they are followers rather than leaders. It stands to reason that they develop a need to care for others so they will be cared for, and a fear of separation and loneliness. In contrast, boys favor independence, separation and freedom, and it is attachments that make them anxious.

And so the model is established early on: The female is dependent, eager to please and frightened of being left. And the male is independent, expects to be pleased and feels suffocated by attachments.

FAMILY DYNAMICS THAT ENCOURAGE THE PLEASER

In addition to basic socialization experiences, there are some dynamics that exist in families that can lead to or add to a woman's need for approval. I've isolated the most common of these to show some of the contributing factors. One or more of these scenarios may sound familiar to you. Perhaps the story inside your family matches one of the following profiles, but it has never before occurred to you that these dynamics might have had such an impact on your adult attitudes.

The Violent Home

There was always a lot of fighting between Alice's parents, and this scared her. She never understood what the reasons were—it seemed that her father had the volcanic ability to erupt into anger without warning. Sometimes the fights reached a fever pitch. Once Alice's father twisted her mother's arm so hard that he sprained it.

Early on, Alice figured out that the best way to avoid becoming a target in the fighting was to stay out of sight and remain as quiet as possible. That way, her father could not fault her with the outspoken behavior that seemed to get her mother into so much trouble.

She decided that her mother must be doing something wrong—otherwise why would he be so mad all the time? Alice resented her mother for that. She vowed that when she grew up and got married, she would be loving and quiet. She never wanted to be responsible for provoking this kind of rage in a man.

Alice felt that the way to avoid trouble in relationships was to be both invisible and caring at the same time. She developed the attitude at a young age that men must be soothed and catered to.

It's very easy for young children to develop misunderstandings about important matters if their parents don't make a concerted effort to communicate directly about what's really going on. Alice's parents would probably have been very surprised to hear the conclusions she reached about their fighting. But they did not think to clarify the situation, and the seeds were planted early on for Alice to become a pleaser in her later relationships with men. She couldn't bear the idea that the horrible scenes from her childhood might be replayed in her own relationships.

The Absent Mother

The role of the pleaser also develops in the fertile ground of a family where the mother is nonfunctional for one reason or another. She might be an alcoholic or mentally unbalanced, she might be physically ill or disabled, or she might be unavailable because she is forced or chooses to work long hours outside the home. In any case, in this scenario it is common for a young girl to take on the role of mother as her way of trying to hold the family together. She does it, basically, to make a frightening situation feel safer for herself, but in the process she learns to focus on caring for others rather than on developing herself as a person.

From ages ten to seventeen, Gloria Steinem lived alone with her mentally ill mother. In the story "Ruth's Song" from her book *Outrageous Acts and Everyday Rebellions* (Holt, Rinehart and Winston, 1983), she talks about having to take over the mother role:

> She was just a fact of life when I was growing up; someone to be worried about and cared for; an invalid who lay in bed with eyes closed and lips moving in occasional responses to voices only she

could hear; a woman to whom I brought an endless stream of toast and coffee, bologna sandwiches and dime pies, in a child's version of what meals should be. She was a loving, intelligent, terrorized woman who tried hard to clean our littered house whenever she emerged from her private world, but who could rarely be counted on to finish one task. In many ways, our roles were reversed: I was the mother and she was the child. Yet, that didn't help her, for she still worried about me with all the intensity of a frightened mother, plus the special fears of her own world full of threats and hostile voices.

. . . Once, I made one last stab at being a child. By pretending to be much sicker with a cold than I really was, I hoped my mother would suddenly turn into a sane and cheerful woman bringing me chicken soup à la Hollywood. Of course she could not. I stopped pretending.

This role-reversal happened in a very different way with Betty, a successful attorney, and her ten-year-old daughter, Melanie.

In many ways, Betty was the perfect image of a successful and liberated mother. Unfortunately, she was so busy pursuing her career that she failed to see what was happening to Melanie in her absence.

During the period that Betty was working to become a partner at her firm, she often worked long days, well into the evening, leaving her husband, John, and Melanie to fend for themselves. John was initially supportive of her need to work especially hard, but sometimes his patience ran a little thin when things around the house weren't getting done.

Melanie noticed her father's dissatisfaction, and she also felt very uncomfortable with the new lack of structure in their lives. She remembered how peaceful everything had been when her mother was around more. She wondered how she was going to survive without any structure, and she felt compelled to take it upon herself to fill the empty space created by her mother's absence.

Melanie's parents could have reassured her that it was okay for her to continue being a child, that Mommy and Daddy would take care of the house. But they were not sensitive to the way Melanie was affected. Instead, they noticed only that she was being "such a good girl," doing a lot of work around the house, and they praised her for being a big help to them.

Melanie developed a desperate fear of having no guidelines to depend on . . . so desperate that she eventually married a controlling man she didn't even love because he supplied so much structure in her life.

Father's Favorite Girl

Another common family setup occurs when a girl becomes her father's favorite. This happens most often when there are no male children or when the boys turn out to be a disappointment.

The young girl who is favored by her father may seem fortunate because he treats her more like a boy and, in that way, gives her the opportunity to develop independently.

It is true that he does encourage her independence,

but not in the same way as he would a boy. The flavor is different. He encourages her to please him by acting as though she were a confident, achieving son. But often he sets the parameters for her success and withholds praise unless she follows his plan for her to the letter.

Helen's father was a successful medical doctor and when his son, Eric, was born he made no secret of his pride—and bragged that Eric would follow in his footsteps. Helen was two years older than her brother, but he had never voiced any expectations for her—until Eric was diagnosed as having a mild mental disability. Suddenly Helen's father turned his full attention on her.

"Father was a very strong man," Helen says of him now. "Before Eric's disability was discovered, he was my father's favorite child, something I never minded because I knew he loved me, too. It was just that Eric was pushed more in every way than I was.

"Then, later, when Eric couldn't measure up, my father turned all his attention on me. Suddenly, I was the one who was supposed to follow in his footsteps and I found myself being propelled toward medical school without being allowed the consideration of other options. Deep down inside, I knew I was more interested in journalism than I was in medicine, but I was so thrilled with my father's pride in me and his special attention that I covered up my true feelings for a long time."

Finally, during a school break, Helen admitted to her father that she wasn't cut out to be a doctor. "He was furious, and when I explained to him what I really wanted to do, he refused to accept it. I said, 'But, Dad, you said I could be anything I wanted to be.' And he snapped at me, 'Yes, but it's obvious that you don't know what you want.' "

Helen's father encouraged her development *on his terms,* not her own, allowing her only a kind of pseudo-independence. And while she recognized this, she felt addicted to the positive encouragement she received when she did what he wanted and won his approval.

A similar scenario played itself out later in her relationship with her husband. It took Helen many years of therapy before she dared make major decisions without worrying about the approval of the very strong men in her life.

The Dominant Mother

Another environment that encourages women to become pleasers is one in which the mother is very assertive and the father is very passive. Growing up, these young girls often wish their fathers would be stronger and more assertive, and they blame their mothers for preventing the man from taking on more traditional roles. His passivity does not fit with any of the images they have of a father figure and they are embarrassed by it. Often they promise themselves that when they grow up they will not be "too assertive" and thereby keep their man down. They are going to marry a "real man."

In a recent conversation I had with Rhoda, a young

woman frustrated by how this pattern affected her growing-up years, she confessed: "My father was extremely passive . . . he still is. My mother is very aggressive—I'd even call her pushy. My father always did everything she told him to do."

"And you didn't like that?" I asked.

"No," she admitted. "When my mother would make plans and tell him what they were going to do, I sometimes wished that he would just put his foot down and say, 'You go ahead. I'd rather stay home.' "

"You wanted him to be more of a man?"

"Yes, I did."

"Did you ever feel that your father was passive *because* your mother was overbearing?" I asked Rhoda.

"Yes, somewhat."

"Did you ever think about the kind of man you would marry? Did you want someone different from your father?"

"Definitely," Rhoda answered. "I wanted a man who was going to go out and do things . . . be in control of his life. And also someone who would take it upon himself to make plans for us."

"You wanted to be taken care of?" I wondered.

"In a way. My mother always took care of everything. I didn't want to be quite that strong."

Rhoda made her wish come true by marrying a man who needed to control everything in their relationship. At the time we spoke, Rhoda was uncertain about a recent decision she had made to give up her career as a freelance writer to work in his computer-services office. By becoming a pleaser, she suspected she was losing herself.

THE FAMILY INFLUENCE

You can see how any inequity in the power balance in your parents' relationship might have had the affect of moving you in the direction of becoming a pleaser.

But there are three characteristics of the family setup—apart from the way your parents related to each other—that may also have influenced you.

— Were you from a large family?
— Was your home very traditional?
— Was there strict discipline?

If you answered yes to even one of those questions, it is likely that you have identified another factor in your Me Phobia.

The Large Family

In a large family with more than five children, there is a tendency for parents to rely on one or more of the girl children as stand-in mothers. The boys are usually given more freedom to pursue activities outside the home, but the sheer necessity of all the work that has to be done in a large family often traps one or two of the girls in the role of substitute mother.

"I was the second oldest in a family of eight children," Joanne told me. "Throughout my growing-up years, it seemed as though there was always a baby on the way or a new baby that demanded attention. Somehow it fell on me to do most of the pitching in. My brothers never helped—it was just assumed that they were incapable of holding a crying baby or changing a diaper.

"Looking back, I realize that I never resented all the extra work I did to help my mother. Both my parents praised me a lot and held me up as an example. I was the 'perfect daughter' and I enjoyed the role. It made me feel good about myself to know they thought I was so important.

"I remember, though," Joanne continued, "that as I grew older and wanted to be out more, I wasn't as happy about how much my mother depended on me. I still remember one time when I was seventeen years old. My mother had just had another baby—her last, as it turned out—and she was feeling weak. She wanted me to stay home and help her but I *really* wanted to go out. We argued about it and I ended up going, but she was pretty cool to me for a couple days. And that made me feel just terrible. I never argued with her about leaving the house again."

Like most girls raised in this environment, Joanne developed a reliance on pleasing to get along in the world, and this reliance carried over into her later relationships with men.

The Traditional Family

More traditional families tend to teach their children role expectations that are based on what they see as clear-cut gender differences. Boys are meant to interact with the outside world, manage the money and discipline the children. Girls are taught the household tasks, the interpersonal skills, and (most important of all) that pleasing their man is a top priority.

A friend of mine remembers how true this was in her family, where traditional attitudes—including religious training—seemed to reinforce the feeling that women were second-class citizens. "The worst thing imaginable to my mother was that she wouldn't have dinner ready when my father came home from work," Carrie said, laughing. "And he wasn't a bad man, either. He expected her to cater to him because that was the way it was supposed to be. He loved her, though."

"Do you think your mother was happy?" I asked Carrie.

"Happiness wasn't a concept my mother understood. She didn't think she had a right to it, so she never thought about it. I know she got a lot of consolation from her religion. But when I was older, she once said something that gave me a clue to how she felt. When I was thinking of getting married, she warned me that I would have to be ready to make sacrifices because that's just the way things work for women. I felt so sad for her. I thought, 'Not me! I'll never be like that.' But in the five years of my marriage, I reminded myself so much of my mother that it frightened me. When I found myself deferring to my husband a lot and worrying about what he thought of me, I sometimes looked at my face in the mirror and said, 'Where did this come from?' I felt that I didn't know myself at all."

"Were you afraid you were becoming like your mother?"

"It seemed that way, in spite of my determination not to be like her. I figured out later that I didn't like the way she was, but all the learning was deeply ingrained in me and it was bound to surface."

The Strict Family

In a very strict family with rigid rules, girls and boys alike often live in terror of what will happen if they make a false move. Boys, however, seem to be able to escape more easily into parentally sanctioned activities outside the family, while girls are forced to face more interactions with the strict and often punitive parent(s). As a result, they become very good at guessing parental expectations and then pleasing, since it is better than risking punishment and disapproval.

"My father was in the military and sometimes our house felt like boot camp," Cheryl told me. "He was especially tough on my brother because he was very into this macho stuff for boys. It wasn't hard at all for me to figure out that I could win his pleasure by being sweet and agreeable. I enjoyed the fact that he approved of me, and it saved me from getting some of the grief my brother got. Of course, my mother was very submissive—how could she not be with a man like him?

"Things got a little touchy when I started dating. My father was the type who would practically want a formal investigation of each boy who took me out—my dates hated coming to our house. Sometimes I would be embarrassed, but I figured out a way to sweet-talk him into letting me go places. As long as he saw me as his innocent little girl who would never do anything bad, we got along fine."

I asked Cheryl if this pattern repeated itself in any of her relationships. She nodded. "It was automatic for me to do a sweet little girl routine to get my way. If I was interested in a man, I'd throw on the switch and I think a lot of men found me charming and adorable. But the routine never worked for long—they'd get bored with it. It took me a lot of years to wise up."

LOOKING BACK

Now that you've begun to think about your growing-up years and how they might have contributed to your Me Phobia, I'd like to ask you to take it one step further and try to pinpoint how much these experiences might have contributed to your current pleasing problem. Take a few minutes to answer the following questions about your youth with a yes or no and find your score.

1. Did you play outside as much as you did indoors?
   ____ Yes ____ No

2. Did you help your father as much as your mother?
   ____ Yes ____ No

3. Did you receive an allowance? ____ Yes ____ No

4. Did you play with toys other than those "made for girls"? ____ Yes ____ No

5. Did you have a close relationship with an independent woman? ____ Yes ____ No

6. Did you read about or hear about independent women? ____ Yes ____ No

7. Were you encouraged to think about or express your opinions about current events? ____ Yes ____ No

8. If you had brothers, did you have the same curfew at the same ages? ____ Yes ____ No (Leave blank if you had no brothers.)

9. Were you encouraged to learn to drive when you came of age? ____ Yes ____ No

10. Did you feel you could be anything you wanted to be when you grew up? ____ Yes ____ No

11. Did you ever travel out of town alone by bus, train or plane? ____ Yes ____ No

12. Did you ever hitchhike? ____ Yes ____ No

13. Did you work to earn money? ____ Yes ____ No

14. Did you generally shop by yourself or with friends for your clothes? ____ Yes ____ No

15. Would you keep a date with a girlfriend if a boy you liked asked you out for the same evening? ____ Yes ____ No

16. Was your mother an "independent woman"? ____ Yes ____ No

17. Did your father relate to most women as equals? ____ Yes ____ No

18. Did you have a fairly carefree childhood, unburdened by adult responsibilities? ____ Yes ____ No

19. Did you participate in competitive sports? ____ Yes ____ No

20. Did you have the use of a car in high school? ____ Yes ____ No

SCORING

Count up your no answers and find the description that matches below:

— Fifteen or more no answers indicates a high potential for Me Phobia. Your upbringing clearly socialized you to please.

— Seven to fourteen no answers indicates some potential for Me Phobia, with your upbringing being
one of the influences in your need to please.
— Six or fewer no answers indicates a low potential
for Me Phobia. Your upbringing played a minor
role in your need to please.

Now that you better understand how the conditioning factors in your growing-up years might have led
to your need to please, let's move on to step five in
your recovery. In the next chapter we will examine
why you fall into—and stay in—relationships that
make you suffer so much and rob you of your self-
esteem.

6

THE JOURNEY FROM
ECSTASY TO AGONY

How many times have you heard women say, "He just swept me off my feet and before I knew it, I was involved with him"? Maybe you've said it yourself.

Are you scared that you seem to have no power to resist a certain type of man—that even while your head is warning you away, your heart is careening you forward?

Do you regret the way you "followed your heart," as the initial thrill of the relationship wears off? Do you try to change things, maybe believing promises from your mate about new behavior that never materializes? Does it feel like a vicious cycle—the more you try to change him, the worse he gets?

You may be surprised to learn that there are patterns in relationships like yours. In fact, every relationship between a controlling man and a compliant woman goes through predictable stages.

Step five of your recovery involves looking at the stages in the development of your relationship. By doing this, you will begin to see more clearly why things have reached the present state. And if you are now in the early stages of a relationship that already shows signs of trouble, you will have a chance to change your own behavior to avoid the pitfalls that otherwise lie ahead.

In this chapter, I will help you look at:

— How something so potentially destructive gets started in the first place.
— How and when the problems begin to show themselves.
— What kinds of efforts men and women commonly make to keep things from falling apart.

The stages of your relationship with a controlling man usually follow this pattern:

Before the Fall is the mind-set you're in prior to the time you choose your man. And for women who fall for controlling men, this is usually a vulnerable period. The second stage, *Falling in Love,* is the initial attraction and commitment. The third stage, which I call *Budding Resentments,* begins as one or both of you become aware that there is inequity in your relationship. The next stage is the full-blown *Power Struggle* where both of you try to get your way, using the manipulative maneuvers described earlier. In *Negotiating Strategies,* you try to conscientiously work on the relationship to prevent it from ending.

And, in the final stage, you reach some kind of *Accord* or decide upon *Termination* of the relationship.

As you read through the descriptions of these stages, you may feel as though you have gone through some of them more than once. Chances are, you have. Maybe you negotiated the stages and reached some kind of accord a few years back. But then, circumstances changed and you found the budding resentments raising their ugly heads again. This might have led to a resumption of the power struggle, new negotiations and a new accord—or, this time, termination of the relationship.

In reality, the stages can occur many times during the course of a relationship. Small battles can add up to form the major power struggle that is always bound to exist between a controlling man and a compliant woman. This struggle involves your drive to win his love by pleasing him and his fear that, in giving you that love, he will lose control. For him, losing control is dangerous—a sign that he is unmanly or dependent in some way. He can't stand the idea that you might somehow achieve an upper hand and possibly end the relationship.

STAGE ONE: BEFORE THE FALL

Before you've even met the controlling man who seems to steal your heart, there are certain life situations that tend to make you more vulnerable in your attraction to him.

Emily described this kind of situation when she

came to see me last year. Two years earlier, she had met Ben.

It was a difficult time for her. She was unhappy with her job and was just beginning to realize that she would have to go back to school for an advanced degree if she was going to go further in her career. There wasn't much support from her family, since her parents were preoccupied with financial problems.

Ben came along at that time and he was so persistent in his courting that Emily felt carried away on the tide of his determination. By the time she realized that she didn't really want to marry Ben, it took a tremendous amount of energy to turn him away. One night, he camped on her doorstep just to talk to her. Finally, in desperation, Emily asked her brother to come and stay with her and help head Ben off. Together they managed to end the relationship, but the struggle left Emily feeling even weaker and more vulnerable than she had felt when she first met Ben.

"When George came along, my resistance was pretty low," she said, speaking of the man she married six months later. "In retrospect, I see that he was exactly the same kind of man as Ben—just as controlling, just as demanding. But by then, I was too tired to fight and I was too embarrassed to ask my brother to help me again. I gave in and married him, even though I knew deep down that it wasn't right."

Like many women, you may have fallen into your relationship with a controlling man because he appeared at a time when you were feeling particularly insecure. It's easier to fall in love when you're needy than when you're feeling strong and good about yourself. Maybe you resist giving up a "sure thing" because you fear being alone. Or you might simply feel too weak to fight a persistent suitor.

Over the years, your focus has always been on the needs of others, and this has left you ill-prepared to meet and evaluate crises in your own life. You may unconsciously respond to life transitions (particularly the ending of attachments) by becoming involved with a controlling man. "He will solve the problems . . . he will make my anxieties go away. All I need to do is please him and everything will be fine."

Susan admits that she married Stephen for this reason. When she met him, she was newly divorced and Stephen was her lawyer. At that time, Susan's life was in upheaval. Not only was she on her own for the first time at age forty-two, but she had just finished chemotherapy treatment for uterine cancer and she felt very shaky and unattractive. Stephen's wisdom, love, and concern seemed to cover her like a warm, safe blanket. She was relieved that a man could find her desirable enough to want to take care of her. Susan prospered under Stephen's care and they were married one year after her divorce.

Soon Susan began to feel stronger, both emotionally and physically. She grew to resent the way Stephen controlled everything about their lives. At the time she came to see me she was feeling stifled and angry. "He actually gives me a list of things to do every day before he leaves for work," she complained. "And he calls me during the day to find out if I've done them."

In Susan's case, her relief at having someone take care of her during a vulnerable period turned to resentment when she grew stronger. Her gratitude toward him for the way he had helped her stifled her feelings and, as her anger grew, so did her guilt and frustration.

Sometimes your vulnerability can be the result of outside influences. Maybe you feel insecure because family members are putting pressure on you to marry. Lately the Harvard-Yale Study added pressure to the lives of many single women over thirty by proposing that their prospects of marriage were quite grim. After that study was published, many women called in to my radio show to ask if I thought they should "settle" for the man they were currently involved with since their chances of finding someone better seemed so remote.

Now, think back to the time you made the commitment to the man in your life. What were your pressures? Maybe you weren't even aware that you were under any particular stress. But ask yourself: Did the relationship soften the impact of some other significant things that were happening?

Think back now and use the following checklist to analyze your stress level around the time of your commitment.

Stress Checklist

(Check all of those events that took place during the year before your commitment.)

_____ Death of a parent
_____ Divorce or separation
_____ Death of a close family member
_____ Illness of a parent or close family member

_____ Graduation from school (high school, college, graduate school)

_____ Major injury or illness

_____ Change in job

_____ Major change in financial situation

_____ Death of a close friend

_____ Change in residence

_____ Revision of personal habits

_____ Parents' divorce

_____ Loss of important friend (fight, moved away, etc.)

_____ Pressure to marry

Any one of these factors may have placed you under great pressure—and maybe several of them occurred at the same time in your life. It is well known, for example, that the death of a parent is considered to be one of the most stressful situations a person can encounter. But your stress might also have been the result of a more "benevolent" event—like graduating from college or moving to a new job or city.

By looking back at what was going on at the time of your commitment, you may see that you were feeling particularly vulnerable and that your weakness played a big part in your decision about the man in your life.

If you are now thinking about making a commitment to a man who you realize depends on many of the controlling maneuvers in the second chapter, examine the Stress Checklist as it relates to you now. You will become much more aware of the need for security that may be affecting your feelings about him.

The pressures and concerns that I've noted here can lay the groundwork for your susceptibility to involvement with a controlling man. There are several reasons for this:

1. You are preoccupied with other stresses and don't notice the warning signs of trouble in the relationship.
2. You see the signs but either consciously or unconsciously welcome the idea of having someone to depend on.
3. You use the relationship to escape from your other pressures and don't pay much attention to whether or not he is the right person for you.

Sometimes the feelings of insecurity lie so far under the surface that you don't even realize you have them. When Geri met Frank, she was in her senior year of college and felt her life was going pretty well. In reality, Geri harbored a deep-seated terror of what she was going to face once she was pushed out into the world.

During her growing-up years, Geri had always been shy and she had trouble making friends. She envied some of the girls she knew who seemed to move so easily through social situations. Geri's shyness made her feel insecure and less likable than her more assertive friends. When she first went away to college, she was scared to death that she wouldn't meet people. But then she joined a sorority and things changed.

Geri's sorority became like a family to her. She was accepted there and gradually began to feel more comfortable and liked by others. During those four years, she developed deep attachments to the sorority gang. When she was with the other members, she felt really good about herself for the first time in her life.

At the beginning of her senior year, some of this confidence began to slip away as she realized that her sorority life would soon be over. She couldn't admit it even to herself, but Geri was really panic-stricken about having to be on her own. Her images of the future were vague at best.

Then, in the nick of time, Frank arrived to supply an alternative. Frank was a very self-confident young man and Geri admired his certainty about the direction he was headed in. She looked up to him as being someone she could never hope to be.

During Geri's last year of college, she and Frank became closer and closer, but Geri was uncomfortable because there had been no talk of a future together. She began to initiate discussions about marriage and finally, to her great relief, Frank proposed.

Geri never stopped to think about whether she really loved this man enough to spend the rest of her life with him. That didn't seem to matter. What did matter was that Frank was willing to take care of her and provide her with sure-fire protection against the unknown and frightening future.

While all of this was going on, Geri was hardly aware of what she was trying to avoid through her relationship. It wasn't until many years later, after she had ended what had become a miserable marriage, that she began to recognize the role her fear of change had played in her marriage to Frank. As C.S. Lewis once said, "When the most important things in our life happen, we quite often do not know, at the moment, what is going on."

Rachel is another example of this. At twenty-three, she still lives at home with her parents while she works to raise money for her own apartment. Meanwhile, she has become involved with Ron, a man she met through her work. Rachel enjoys Ron's company and they have a lot in common, but she has a very strong sense that she needs to experience some independence before she gets married—to Ron or to any man. That's the reason she's saving money for her own apartment.

But lately, Rachel has found herself staying at Ron's apartment more and more. She has even moved some of her things in. The more comfortable this arrangement becomes, the less enthusiastic Rachel feels about forging out on her own.

Rachel doesn't realize that she is using her relationship with Ron to avoid facing her fear of leaving home and really growing up. If she is fortunate, circumstances will somehow force her to have that living-on-her-own experience before she makes a firm commitment. After being on her own, she may discover that Ron isn't the man for her. In any case, whatever she decides, she'll know that she didn't commit to him as a way of escaping her fears.

In my interviews with women, I've found one element in particular to be a common thread running through the events that are taking place around the time they make commitments to controlling men. That element is *freedom*. In some way, most of these women are being released from a past attachment and are facing the unknown. And the smell of freedom makes them anxious rather than exhilarated. This anxiety causes them to create new situations of bondage in relationships with controlling men. These are solutions that they often live to regret but that, at the time, seem safer than no attachment at all.

Freedom is frightening if you have Me Phobia. Accustomed to pleasing others, this new opportunity to look at yourself, to begin to know yourself, and to meet your own needs brings up much anxiety.

Now we come to the moment of attraction or falling in love. Both your early conditioning and your psychological susceptibility have sensitized you to fall for a controlling man.

STAGE TWO: FALLING IN LOVE

Falling in love is wonderful. And for a compliant woman and a controlling man, this is probably the best time in your relationship. That's not because you love each other more in the beginning. *It's because you know each other the least.* The ecstasy you feel has more to do with the *expectations* you have than with any real knowledge of each other. You believe that this man will magically heal any of the psychological wounds you have. He probably feels the same way about you.

I have a friend who is always falling in love at a moment's notice. Last month she returned from a skiing vacation flushed and happy. "I'm in love," she declared. "Tom is the man I've always wanted."

Aware that my friend had only spent two days

with this man, I asked, "How can you say that about a person you've just met?"

She had an answer that made perfect sense to her, if not to me. "Our chemistry is so perfect. We were instantly attracted."

Later, when she found out that the man of her dreams was married, she couldn't believe she hadn't seen the signs. "I really felt as though I knew everything about him," she wailed.

But how could she? Love develops from a knowledge and understanding of a person. It's something that can't happen in two days. What my friend was really in love with were her own expectations and dreams, rather than the real person.

It's easy to fall in love with a controlling man if you are a woman who has always concentrated on pleasing others. You may feel that a part of you is missing, but you see that he seems more complete and you believe that you can find what's missing in you through your association with him.

It might surprise you to know that one thing that attracts you to a controlling man is his ability to get angry. Anger is a feeling you've probably always had trouble expressing. Either you've tried to repress it altogether, or it has come out in inappropriate bursts. Most likely anger was a dangerous emotion to express when you were growing up.

These deep needs—to be taken care of so you can remain passive, and to have someone else express the anger you have repressed—are the bases for the chemistry, for the sparks that ignite when a compliant woman meets a controlling man.

The controlling man is at his most charming during

this stage. He is working to get something he wants—
you. And he is good at seduction. Placed in a situation where you want to be loved, you become more
than usually anxious to please. You may not even
notice that your relationship has started off on an
unequal footing. Or you may notice it but feel that it's
of no real consequence.

Looking back on the early stages of her relationship, Diane recalls, "He was so sure of himself, so
dedicated to his career when we first met. We lived
in different cities and he would call me on Thurs-
days to plan our weekend. I would wait for his call,
and when we got together, it was fabulous. He did
it up right—really swept me off my feet. When he
couldn't make it for the weekend, I'd try to fill up
my time somehow—it was totally up to him whether
or not we could get together. I never turned him
down. I didn't want to cause any ripples in such a
terrific relationship."

During this stage in the relationship, a controlling
man will usually lead you to believe that anything
about him that might be construed as negative will
automatically be fixed by virtue of his relationship
with you. After all, you are so loving and giving. In
that way he gives you a tremendous high and a feeling of power. It's what you have always wanted—the
opportunity to help someone through your love.

As Diane says, "When I saw his apartment for the
first time, I was horrified. I had never seen such a
mess. All his clothes were on the floor . . . one pile for
clean and one pile for dirty. There were roaches in
the kitchen. He never asked me to clean up, but I
started helping out little by little. I just couldn't stand
the filth. When I cleaned, he'd tell me how happy that

made him . . . how he had always wanted to live a more orderly life, but up until now, he'd never been motivated in that direction. I thought I was going to help him do that, but I'm still picking up everything. I guess I never loved him enough or the right way, because he never changed." Clearly, Diane misinterpreted his real "need" or the reasons behind his controlling behavior. She assumed that his behavior was directly related to her actions.

The controlling man will also exhibit jealousy at this stage, and this too may give you a high. You don't see it as a controlling maneuver; rather it seems to be proof of his strong feelings for you. In trying to please him, you are willing to give up or change some of your ways. Maybe you see your friends less, or change your style of clothing. You're unconcerned by these changes because his love is more than a fair trade-off.

When you are caught up in falling in love with a controlling man, the inequities that emerge in the relationship do not concern you very much. On the contrary, in some ways you are comforted by them.

STAGE THREE: BUDDING RESENTMENTS

"When we were going out together before we got married, I ignored a lot of things about Matt," admitted Pamela, who came to see me about her marital problems. "He drank too much, and I know he dated other women. I saw it, but I denied it to myself. I was too attracted to him. When he asked me to marry him, I remember having a nagging little doubt that maybe I shouldn't do this, but I was also thrilled that he had chosen me. At first, after we married, things were okay, but now he sometimes comes home late and I know he's been out drinking or with another woman.

"The thing that really gets me is that, while he's out having a great time, I'm home taking care of his daughter from his first marriage. He expects this and I think it's rotten."

I asked Pamela if she had confronted Matt with her resentment, and she shook her head. "I can't stand the thought of becoming one of those bitchy wives who is always nagging. That's why Matt left his first wife. I keep trying to figure out if there's some other way to change things."

It might take two weeks, or two months, or two years . . . or maybe as long as twenty years. But eventually, you begin to see the inequity in your relationship.

You notice that he has more freedom in the relationship. You ask yourself, "Why do I have to be home for him when he wants me . . . and yet he feels free to go out when he knows I am going to be home." *Click.* An awareness begins.

You notice that you often ask him for permission when you want to do things—and that he assumes that his decisions speak for both of you. *Click.*

You realize that while you may write the checks, he makes the major money decisions—and he doesn't give you very much information about how much money you've saved or what your investments are. *Click.*

You discover that no matter how hard you try to please him, he continues to find fault with you. *Click.*

You see his take-charge attitude in sharp contrast to your own what-can-I-do-to-help approach. *Click.*

Your awareness of the inequities begins to make you feel frustrated—especially because he doesn't seem to appreciate the fact that you do things for him. Notes Diane, who still cleans up after her messy husband, "I would be happy doing anything for him, if only he appreciated it."

You also begin to be aware that this man of your dreams is not going to be able to meet your needs. He's not holding up his end of the bargain. You thought the deal was that you would please him and he would give you love and security in return. But now it's clear that the the trade-off is not working.

There are a number of things that can happen to bring these inequities to light. The first, and most common, is the passage of time. The bloom leaves the rose, the romantic glow fades, and reality sets in. You see him and yourself more clearly, as well as how you relate. You become a little less consumed with pleasing him because he has now made a commitment to you and you are less afraid of losing him.

Another thing that can happen is that you get over the vulnerability that led to your attraction in the first place. Once the crisis has passed and your self-esteem begins to mend, you aren't so needy. When you were weak, it felt as though you were swimming with the tide—it was easy. But when you are stronger and try to swim against the tide, it's clearer how controlling your man is. And you begin to resent the ways in which he tries to control you.

A third possibility is that something happens to him that shifts the power balance in the relationship. A disruption in the status quo causes you to become more aware of what has existed all along. Maybe he loses his job . . . or comes into a lot of family money.

Whether the change is good or bad, it can cause you to focus on things about the relationship that you have taken for granted before or not paid much attention to.

When Lynn's live-in boyfriend lost his top-paying job at a local newspaper, their relationship suddenly changed. Although the layoff wasn't due to any incompetency on his part, Derrick was stunned and defeated by the event. "I understood how miserable he was," says Lynn. "That job was his whole life. But after a couple of weeks, I noticed that he was treating me differently. We were living off my income and he really resented it. I laughed it off, telling him, 'Hey, what's mine is yours and vice versa,' but it didn't help. He started accusing me of trying to control him and he'd make nasty cracks about me being the boss. It was intolerable. Eventually I had to admit to myself that Derrick was only happy with me if he felt more important and stronger. And I asked myself, 'Is this love?'"

Whatever the reason for your growing awareness, it leaves you feeling unhappy and frustrated. You feel let down and unappreciated, and you can't understand why your man does not treat you better. Why can't he express his appreciation?

There are a number of reasons he cannot give you the appreciation you feel you deserve:

— He expects to be in the dominant role. Why should he thank you for doing what is expected of you, which is being submissive to him.
— In his mind, it's a fair exchange. He gives you a lot in return. Maybe he feels that he gives you more than you give him.

— If he expresses appreciation, it will bring the unequal arrangement out in the open and perhaps you'll start asking for more. (This is like the slave-master mentality. Keep the subservient person down by making her feel that she hasn't been quite satisfactory.)

— If he openly expresses appreciation, it will be the same as admitting that he needs what you have to give. That admission might give you power over him.

Another thing that happens at this stage in the relationship is that you begin to envy his life-style. You recognize that the relationship is unequal and that he has more freedom. And you resent this.

In her book *Jealousy—Why We Feel It. How to Overcome It* (Morrow, 1985), Nancy Friday discusses this kind of envy.

We are familiar enough with the housebound wife who envies what she imagines to be her husband's freedom to go out into the world every day . . . she lashes out at him: "You aren't watering the plants right." "Why don't you rinse the dishes better?" "Look at these peaches you bought; they've got blemishes on them."

A woman dependent on a man cannot afford open anger. Nagging is what slips out from under the lid she has put on her envy of his power over her.

As your resentment and envy grow, maybe you ask: "How can I make him express his appreciation and love for me?" But the very nature of a relationship with a controlling man is that he cannot give you the support you're looking for—he feels this would shift the power balance and place him in a weaker position. So he stands firm, and the problems escalate into a full-fledged *Power Struggle*—the next stage.

STAGE FOUR: THE POWER STRUGGLE

Your early romantic expectations have been dashed. You feel cheated, betrayed. Having created an ideal picture of your man, you are angry that he has failed to fit that ideal. Now you begin in earnest the struggle to get him to be the man you thought you fell in love with.

When he sees that you disapprove of his behavior, the controlling man escalates the power struggle because he wants to maintain his influence. He doesn't like the fact that you are openly expressing dissatisfaction. He becomes afraid that you might leave him.

In the initial phase of the power struggle, the maneuvers are usually more benign—your man starts with charm, sex, and protection. You may counter with passive behavior or escape. It is usually when these don't work (and we have discussed earlier why they don't) that things escalate into more dramatic responses. And each escalation on the part of one partner usually provokes a more intense reaction from the other. The escalation of the power struggle usually goes from subtle to direct, but it can also go from benignly subtle to hostiley subtle . . . or from benignly direct to hostiley direct.

As people become more and more frightened, their actions are motivated by desperation rather than by clear thinking.

One kind of maneuvering can lead to another without a second thought if the person is angry or frightened enough. And I really believe that fear underlies even the most violent controlling behavior.

During the power struggle, you tend to fall back on the same maneuvers you used as a child when you weren't getting what you needed from your parents or caretakers. Maybe you ran from the situation, or threw a temper tantrum, or withdrew, or became defiant, or just tried to be as "good" as you possibly could. These patterns are deeply ingrained and they tend to emerge when you feel threatened as an adult.

At the same time as these maneuvers are used to protect you from getting hurt even more, they also serve to further cut you off from the intimacy you desire. By this stage in your relationship, you're feeling very rejected and lonely.

The more often Jess was late getting home from work, the more Carol feared that he was having an affair with another woman. She protected herself from these fears by becoming increasingly critical of him. He responded to this criticism by becoming resentful. "She can't control me," he said, and he began to stay out even later. But sometimes he was lonely; after several weeks he began to get tired of playing this game. When he met Margery in a bar one evening, he thought, "Well, if I'm going to be accused of having an affair, I might as well have one."

Carol could remember how she pressured her father in the same way to stay home and stop drinking. When she was only six, she gave him a lecture about how irresponsible he was to leave the family in the evenings. Now here she was, caught in the same pattern.

It's easy to get stuck in a power struggle. Maybe it seems more logical to sit down and try to talk it out, but this is hard to do because you're both afraid that if you stop to take a good, honest look at the situation, you'll get hit from behind by your partner. So the motto of this stage becomes: "Stay alert and on the defensive."

In spite of the standoff, you will probably reach a point where you will try to negotiate your differences to prevent the breakup that will begin to seem inevitable.

STAGE FIVE: NEGOTIATING STRATEGIES

There are many different events that set the stage for negotiations. Often these events are dramatic— somewhere along the way, a line gets crossed and an awakening takes place that tells you your relationship is in such big trouble that something must be done. Examples of these events might be:

— The threat that one or the other of you is going to leave.
— A physical illness, accident or near-death experience.
— A religious experience.
— An act of violence or suicide attempt.
— A separation.

Often the most fruitful negotiations occur after a separation, because both of you are motivated to try and get back together. You're unhappy without each other and you decide to try again. Since you've been apart, a little of the romantic ecstasy that you felt when you were falling in love is reactivated and it oils the machinery, lending some much-needed good feelings to the process of reconciliation.

There are common ways that couples try to negotiate resolutions to their struggles. These attempts to negotiate can take place without an outside person (such as a therapist or a clergyman), but they're more likely to be successful if a professional is used. Why? A third party can supply the needed accountability and objectivity. And you'll tend to feel more trusting that your partner isn't trying to trick you.

Two negotiating strategies that usually *don't* work are establishing trade-offs or having general discussions about the relationship. When you set up a system of trade-offs ("If you do this for me, I'll do this for you"), you are giving the relationship what I call a "vanity fix." The underlying difficulties are not addressed. And a general discussion of "what's wrong with this relationship" rarely allows the objectivity needed to address the situation honestly.

Some couples reach the negotiating stage many times during their relationship. After each power struggle they try desperately to put things in balance but they fail to address their underlying fears, and the endless cycle builds into a long history of lies and hurts.

Elaine and Michael believed they were approaching their negotiations in a healthy and honest manner when they decided to take the lead from an article they read in *Ms.* magazine called "How to Write Your Own Marriage Contract." Elaine was upset about the inequities in the relationship. She did everything around the house, took care of remembering birthdays, and made all the social arrangements. She felt that Michael should play more of a role in this. He agreed that he was willing to work on it, and, with high hopes, they sat down and began to divide up the family responsibilities.

A month later Elaine sat in my office in tears. "Why didn't it work?" she cried. "He seemed so agreeable, but it lasted about a week. Then things just went back to the way they were."

"Why do *you* think it didn't work?" I prodded. "Do you have any ideas about that?"

"It looks like he never meant it in the first place," she said angrily. "Like he was just trying to appease me."

"You think he tricked you?"

"I don't know why it all fell apart."

What began to emerge was that the real conflict between Elaine and Michael was deeply buried. By dealing with the surface issues of who performed what tasks around the house, they were merely avoiding the true reasons for the power struggle: Mi-

chael's need to control Elaine and her desperate desire to please him at any cost.

A lot of game playing goes on in the negotiating
stage because both of you want the relationship back
on an even keel, and you may use the same controlling and counter-controlling maneuvers that got you
into trouble in the first place. Resolutions are bound
to fail when they are built on the same false hopes
and expectations you had when you started the
relationship.

Usually the negotiations break down in one of four
ways. Sometimes the promises made were never
meant to be kept. They were only maneuvers de-
signed to get the relationship going again.

Negotiations also break down when one of the
partners (usually the woman, especially if she's a
pleaser) ends up doing all the giving in, feeling a
sudden panic about the possibility of losing the other.

Sometimes promises are made impulsively and are
not thought out. In the harsh light of day, they don't
hold up.

Finally, if a separation has occurred and the couple
tries for a reconciliation, the initial romantic feelings
experienced in being back together can create a false
sense of trust that the problems have been solved—
when in fact, they may never have been discussed at
all.

When negotiations work, they can lead to a new
life together as you and your man begin to act as
partners in healing some of the wounds in your relationship. When negotiations break down, they can
lead to a further stagnation in the relationship—an
uneasy peace. Or other storms can erupt, colored by
new anquish and revenge. In the next two chapters,

we'll look at the reasons women stay trapped in bad relationships . . . and what happens when they reach a breaking point with their controlling men. This understanding will form the second part of step six in your recovery from Me Phobia.

7

WHY DO YOU STAY?

"It's really not so bad."

"I love him ... even when things are at their worst, I still love him."

"Maybe I expect too much ... it's not as if there are a lot of great men out there waiting for me."

"I've been with him so long. What am I supposed to do—throw away everything we've built together?"

"The children come first ... and they need a stable family."

"I just don't care anymore. I'll have to make the best of it."

You've been back and forth in the power-struggle game for years and nothing changes. Why do you stay in a relationship that only promises more bad times ahead?

In my many interviews with women, I've come across situations that make me think, "This sounds intolerable." And I ask them point-blank, "Why do you stay with this man?"

The answer I hear most often is something like this: "When I weigh the pros and cons, it just seems that I have more to lose by leaving than I do by staying." (And P.S. . . . "Maybe he'll change.")

The women I've had these conversations with have ready-made answers for this question. It always strikes me *how much they've thought about leaving.* They've seriously fantasized about what life might hold for them outside the relationship. This process of weighing the pros and cons releases some of the guilt they feel about staying in a relationship that they know is not right for them. Their justification is, "I know this situation will never change, and I probably should have left years ago, *but at least I'm working on it.*" Deep down, these women are avoiding their fears of how *scary* they think it will be for them outside their relationship. They know what it's like inside; outside is a frightening unknown.

Step six in your recovery from Me Phobia is realizing why you stay in a relationship in which the power balance is so severely off-kilter—a relationship that makes you so unhappy.

Think about all the time and energy you spend poring over the bad points in your relationship and trying to uncover slim hopes beneath the brutal truths. Think of the long conversations you have with friends when you really let your hair down and talk about him. Think of the words of dissatisfaction and hurt that fill your journal—if you keep a journal. Or the thousands of dollars you spend spilling your heart out to a therapist.

You may think that you are doing something, that you are in the process of deciding whether to stay or to leave. You don't want to be hasty . . . but is that all that's going on here?

I think not. Take a look at some of the motivations beneath the surface:

1. *You're stalling.* Sometimes stalling tactics are useful—they give you the opportunity to evaluate what's really best for you. But let's face it. Weighing the pros and cons of your relationship for years on end is excessive. Are you using the weighing process to stall?

June's story is a case in point. Long after she felt she wasn't getting anything out of her relationship with Sam, she continued to live with him. When she spoke with me about it, she admitted, "Deep down, I really believe I should leave him—to the point that I fantasize about having a man who will really treat me right."

I asked June, "How does Sam *not* treat you right?"

"It's a little hard to answer that question," she hedged. "Sometimes I'm not sure this really counts as bad behavior. Here's an example. I'll come home from work and say something about my day and he'll get really peeved. He'll say, 'You're always yacking. Can't you give me a little peace?' I know this sounds like a small example, but my feelings are hurt. He doesn't want to talk to me and he isn't that interested in the things that happen at work."

"First of all, it always *counts* if his behavior makes

you feel bad about yourself," I commented. "It looks like you're waiting for something worse to happen before you take action. What is it?"

"If he was having an affair with another woman, it would be easy," June blurted out. "It just seems that I'm making a mountain out of a molehill by thinking about leaving him because of these reasons. Besides, I don't make very much money on my job and I'd rather wait until I can be more financially secure. It's not so bad, really . . ." her voice drifted off wistfully.

"Tell me, how long have you felt this way?"

She shrugged. "Oh, it's been years—maybe ten years."

I looked at June and thought to myself that she would still be with Sam in another ten years—and, worse than that, she would still feel bad about herself—unless she found a way to recognize the validity of her complaints.

2. *You want enough evidence.* Rather than trust your own feelings about your relationship, you feel that you have to collect reams of specific evidence. Your hope is that someday you will have enough proof that you should leave . . . and at that distant time you won't feel so bad about leaving because you'll *know for sure.* In a sense, June was falling into this trap, too. She believed that she didn't really have "a case" against Sam that was good enough to warrant her leaving him. It wasn't enough that he didn't offer her intimacy or companionship. She felt that she needed more hard data to justify her feelings. And she needed him to agree that she had a valid reason for leaving.

A woman who has always concentrated on pleas-

ing her man falls easily into this trap. She doesn't
trust her own feelings enough to know—without evidence—whether the relationship is good or bad. And
she's afraid that if she takes a stand, she will be
called wrong or foolish.

If you're waiting for more evidence before you
make a move, this is a clear symptom of your Me
Phobia. Once again, you're waiting for clear signals
that tell you how to act. You don't know how to
evaluate your own feelings, and you don't trust that
they're on target.

3. *You want to avoid blame.* Many women believe
that they are *the cause* of their man's controlling
behavior . . . that it's something they're doing. Do you
sometimes think it's really all your fault that things
are so rocky? Do you say, "I'm going to do everything
I'm supposed to do, even though it makes me unhappy; at least if the relationship ends, he won't be
able to blame me"?

If you're already feeling bad about yourself, it's
going to be easy for you to take the blame when
things go wrong.

One woman I interviewed for this book confessed
that she couldn't leave her husband for years, even
though he regularly abused her both physically and
emotionally, because she'd already been divorced
twice. "How could I not see this as my fault?" she
asked me. "My other marriages had been a failure. If
this one failed too, I couldn't live with myself."

She finally did leave him when things got so bad
that she felt her daughter was threatened. But she
continued to believe that the failure of the marriage

was more her fault than his. After all, she had choosen the wrong men three times.

You might also want to avoid blame from the outside. A friend of mine was constantly afraid of what her father would say if she left her husband. "He's so proud of the fact that there's never been a divorce in our family. I'm afraid he'd never forgive me if I did this."

Even in this day and age, many women fear the label of "scarlet woman." We have invested so much in being good, and it's sometimes hard to sort out the difference between establishing our rights and behaving in an "immoral" fashion.

4. *You're afraid of your anger.* Maybe you think of anger as a bad thing . . . and it's easy for you to lose the momentum of your anger if he does even one nice thing for you. So you stall, trying to learn how to overcome your negative feelings.

"Last summer we took a vacation that we had been planning for months," Elaine told me. "We'd been having some problems, but I thought this vacation would help us become closer. I dreamed about how nice it would be, just the two of us, walking along the beach and talking. It was going to be a wonderful romantic time and I was hoping we'd talk about moving in together.

"Well, the first thing that happened was that we hooked up with this other couple—it was mostly Jeff's doing. And we spent every waking minute with them. Finally, I got fed up. I was angry because Jeff didn't seem to want to be alone with me. So I confronted him about it and he turned it all around. He said I was being bitchy and overreacting, and what was the matter, didn't I know how to have fun. I shut up after that because I thought he might be right, and besides, I couldn't stand the way he got when I criticized him. It just wasn't worth it.

"For the rest of the vacation, I kept my feelings to myself and pretended to have a good time. But I kept thinking, 'This is it.' I had never felt so cheated and angry.

"A couple weeks after we returned from vacation, Jeff came over one night with a bottle of wine and the pictures from the trip which he had developed. He suggested we spend the evening looking at pictures. At one point, while we were doing this, he put his arm around me and said, 'I'm so glad we did this together. There's nobody I'd rather go on vacation with than you.' I felt all my anger disappear. Later, when I thought back on the vacation, I could only remember that it had been wonderful, even though at the time I was miserable."

Elaine told me she thought this selective memory was very strange, but I explained that her fear of her own anger was so great that she didn't have any way of handling it. When Jeff seemed to make things right between them, she was *relieved* that she no longer had to feel angry, and she was willing to revise the story of their vacation in her own mind so that she wouldn't have a reason to be angry anymore.

5. *You're afraid of the future.* You see the future looming ahead like a scary monster . . . how will you live alone? You say, "I know I'll leave someday when I'm ready," and you practice thinking about being alone. But you never feel quite ready to take the plunge.

There's a lot of talk these days about "settling" for a man because it's so hard to find one in the first place. A woman might say, "He's not great, but at least I have a date for Saturday night." One friend of mine was terrified of being single again because she noted that all her single friends ever talked about was how there weren't any good men out there. "Having Jim is better than being alone," she said.

You might be terrified of being on your own in the world. And you may even tell yourself that someday when you feel stronger about yourself, you'll be able to do it—but not yet, not now.

If your fear of the future is so great that you will remain in a relationship that is sapping your self esteem, chances are that you will never feel strong enough to leave. It's a vicious cycle, but one that is possible to break.

Sometimes you get stuck because you are over-analyzing the relationship. You're in too deep to take an objective look at what's going on. Maybe you're in therapy. Even if you're not, you're probably doing a lot of solo analysis. You think that being aware of your problem is enough. You feel proud of your understanding and believe that you have what it takes to leave any time. In truth, you're just as stuck as the others.

If you've been in the process of weighing the pros and cons of your relationship for a long time, it's time to break free of this circuitous route. Stop trying to be so fair. Give your feelings and perceptions the weight they deserve. Face the knowledge that you already have about what is best for you. If this seems too hard or confusing, later chapters in this book will give you practical ways to begin.

IS LIFE PASSING YOU BY?

Maybe you don't spend a lot of conscious energy evaluating your relationship; instead you just let the tide of life carry you on. You banish the nagging fears and throw yourself into the details of day-to-day living. Somehow it is easier to concentrate on the simple, attainable goals of everyday life—like figuring out what you have to buy at the store or finishing a project at work.

Many women just put off thinking about "the important stuff." As one explained to me, "I just can't waste time worrying about our marraige right now . . . I'm too busy with the kids. And we're renovating our house this summer and that's *taking a lot of energy*. Maybe when all of this is out of the way, I'll have time to think more clearly." I suspect that this woman will never find the time. She doesn't know how (or won't) find that small space for herself, that time to look at her own needs.

Some women escape into activity outside the home. They pour themselves into volunteer work. Or take high-paying jobs where the pressure to achieve lofty goals distracts them from the trouble at home. They're rarely home, and when they are there are a million things to do. They become obsessed with shopping or collecting. They develop crushes on actors, stars, and public figures. The months and years slip by in a whirlwind of activity. They are too busy to really feel the loneliness and emptiness.

Whether you've lost yourself in your children or your work, the fulfillment your experience fills the empty spaces in your relationship and that fullness keeps you unaware of the problem.

Can you identify with these scenarios?

- Do you weigh the pros and cons ad nauseum?
- Are you too caught up in the nitty gritty affairs of daily life?
- Do you escape into the world outside your relationship?
- Finally, do you feel helpless to really figure out what's right for you? Are you afraid of making the wrong choice? Are you paralyzed by the fear that if you leave, you'll lose everything and live the rest of your life in regret?

YOUR REASONS FOR STAYING

Even if, deep down inside, you suspect the truth—that things will never get better and that the only way you're going to have any peace in life is if you leave or if he leaves—while *you* stay, you are giving yourself pretty convincing justifications for staying. See if you recognize yourself in any of these situations:

"It's not really so bad." Maybe you think there are many trade-offs in the relationship. When you add everything up, the positives outweigh the negatives.

You have status (you're a wife), perhaps money, a shared identity, security, companionship. Why give it up when you don't know what else is out there? You might tell yourself that this is all you can expect. You wonder if all men are like this—you might leave him only to find that there's nothing better. This is a sign that you have a serious case of the "brown grass" syndrome. Instead of believing that the grass is always greener, you think just the opposite.

Maybe you no longer remember the way things were when they were good. Or maybe it has always been this way and you're so used to it that you don't notice the way it's deteriorated.

"It's better than nothing." You can't imagine how life without him could possibly be better. You assume that there would be nothing for you without him. And you suspect that others would pity you if you were alone because your own feelings about a single you are so negative.

Think about it for a moment. Even without your man, your house, your children, your job, your clothes, you *are* someone—you're YOU. The roles you play and the external things you use to define yourself are not *you*. So if you're staying for this reason, you should start an immediate campaign to become someone in your own eyes—to see yourself as having rights, as being important and deserving. Only then will you really be able to decide whether or not you should stay. We'll talk about this more in chapter nine.

"I have to think of the children." In spite of the vast number of studies that conclude it is more harmful to

raise children in a destructive environment than with a single loving parent, you still believe that being married is the only way to raise children. No matter how bad things get, you feel your children are better off than they would be if you left. If you are staying for this reason, you're not doing your children any favors. Is this how you want them to grow up? Do you want them to believe that marriage is just a misery that must be endured?

I know a woman who is actively planning to make her "escape" as soon as the children are grown. She spends a lot of time, while her husband is at work, secretly researching places to live and daydreaming about how good it will be when she can be away from him and on her own. Since her youngest child is only five years old, the realization of her dream is many years away. I find it sad that she is willing to live the next fifteen years in a dream instead of having her dream come true now. It's likely that by the time her children are finally grown, she'll be so tired from years of struggling in a bad relationship that she will no longer have the strength to pursue a life of her own. And consider this: Will her children, at age twenty, turn to her and say, "Thank you, Mom, for staying married to Dad for our sake"? I doubt it.

"I'd be throwing my whole life away." You see the years you've spent in the relationship as an invest-ment . . . but it's an investment of dubious value. Instead of thinking about what you would be losing by leaving, think about how much you've already lost by staying so long. What have you given up for him? Your career? Financial independence? Your political ideals? Your individuality? Your personal feelings?

Religion? Freedom to make decisions? Have you been reluctant to speak the truth and really articulate your wants and needs for fear of rocking the boat? You may not even have been consciously aware of the toll these sacrifices have taken in terms of your esteem.

A friend once told me the story of her mother, an immigrant to this country who married an older man when she was only sixteen years old. "He expected her to bow to his wishes in every way," my friend told me sadly. "And she did. While I was growing up, I was constantly aware of how he treated her. He had his own business—a small store—and she worked there every day. Most of the time he was more like a cruel boss to her than he was a loving husband. I know she wasn't happy, but she never considered that there was any other way she could live her life, so she just put up with it.

"She never questioned him, even when he was being unreasonable. I remember how she'd wait all day and not go to the bathroom until she got home because it would take her away from the job for a couple of minutes and he might get angry. She ruined her bladder for him, but she still never complained."

This woman gave up everything, *including her health,* in fear of displeasing her husband. And yet she had grown so used to the situation that it didn't even seem abnormal to her.

"It would hurt him too much if I left him." The husband of one of the women I interviewed had had a terrible loss as a child—his mother had committed suicide and he had been the one to find the body. He told his wife it would kill him to suffer a loss of that magnitude again. She was terrified to end the mar-

riage, even though she was very unhappy. So she stayed and comforted herself with the knowledge that it was her duty . . . until he left her for a younger woman.

Your man may be under a lot of pressure at work or have health problems, and you feel incapable of leaving him in the lurch during these rough times. But a relationship that has sacrifice as its foundation is not healthy. Chances are there will never be a time when it's safe to leave. And maybe you are *really* afraid that if you did leave, you're the one who would be hurt the most.

"I love him." If you believe you love him but you still feel unhappy in the relationship, what is going on? Maybe what you call love is really something else. Think about the phrase, "I love him." Substitute other words for love. You might really be saying, "I need him." Or, "I am grateful to him." Or, "I'm used to him." Or, "I feel sorry for him." When you begin to think about the feelings you're really describing when you talk about love, you will see more clearly what your true motivation is.

I know a woman who is a classic example of someone in love with being in love. She has been seeing a married man for five years. He is quite a bit older than she is, and all along he has made promises to her that one day he'll leave his wife. Of course this has never come to pass. But during the times he's with her, he is the most romantic man alive, showering her with presents and flowers. She tells me, "I'm too much in love with him to leave him, even though it looks like he'll never marry me."

When I ask her to describe the reasons she loves

him, her answers are vague and unfocused. I think what is really going on is that she feels protected by his attentions. As long as she has him, she doesn't have to worry about looking for other relationships. She's safe. But that's not love. Gifts and flowers are not love either, although it's tempting to get caught up in the excitement of a romance.

If this woman really got in touch with her feelings about her relationship with her married lover, I suspect that she would admit that she didn't really feel respected or valued by him.

"I'm not a quitter." It is important to think things through and take some time before you decide to end a relationship, but some couples are engaged in such a terrible power struggle that the loser is defined as the one who caves in and leaves. You might believe that it is weak to leave—better to stay and fight. Or, like one woman I spoke with, you may have had a lot of broken marriages in your family's history and you're determined to be different . . . stronger . . . better. But living together to prove something is not really living.

Maybe you are staying in a bad relationship and don't have a conscious awareness of why you're staying. Years of giving away pieces of yourself, burying your true feelings, and sublimating your desires have numbed you and you live in a state of apathy. You're too tired to fight. You feel listless and bored. Your mind seems to be unable to focus on the true issues. You no longer seem to have any feelings. This state of apathy is a severe warning—the depression can destroy you altogether.

In her novel *Glass People* (Warner Books, 1972), Gail Godwin paints a realistic and scary picture of a woman who is trapped in this kind of apathetic despair:

She . . . padded listlessly about the apartment, opening and closing the refrigerator, stopping to gaze blankly at herself in the oval mirror in the living room. Cameron would not be home for two more hours. What could she do till then? She was not hungry, not particularly sleepy, but she had no energy. Suddenly she remembered the tweezers and went off at once to the medicine cabinet. She got them and returned to the bed. She leaned back on the pillows and crossed one long, pale leg over the other knee. She studied it. It had been two days since she had last tweezed and the hairs were just beginning to return, tiny dark blades tipping up toward the light, barely breaking the skin. If she waited one more day, she could get a better grip on them. But what would she do today? She decided to pluck just a few. With a feeling of anticipation she extricated the first one, just below the kneecap. She held it between the tweezers and looked at it. There it was, root and all. A little white nodule, like wax. Proof of life. Or was it?

This passage dramatizes how deadening the process of living in a relationship with a controlling man can be. This woman had nothing left to ground herself in the world but her listless preoccupations. She'd lost the will to fight.

THE UNDERLYING FEAR

Whether you stay in your relationship because of responsibility, apathy, gratitude or the trade-offs, there is one sure thing at the root of all of these reasons—*fear.*

When you stay because of a belief that it is the responsible thing to do, aren't you really afraid of what other people will think of you if you leave? Aren't you fearful that you won't measure up to their idea of what is right?

Maybe you're staying out of gratitude. "He's done so much for me," or, "He rescued me when I was down." Even in this case you're afraid. It's a fear of what might happen if you stop being grateful. But what is the price you're paying for your gratitude? Trade-offs are never worth it if the price you pay is your self-esteem.

Sometimes it's easier to stay in a situation you know is bad if it also makes you feel like the superior one. If your man is condescending and controlling, for example, it is clear that you are *not* that way. By contrast, you look good to yourself and others. Ask yourself: If you were with someone who was loving, respectful and giving, would you be as confident that you were okay? Maybe your feelings of superiority protect you from the fear that he might leave you. You say, "He's got a good deal and he knows it. Look at how much I put up with." If you were in a relationship with a loving man, you might feel that you didn't deserve him; that it would be easier for another woman to steal him away from you. Of course, your feelings of superiority don't give you any real power in your relationship. They're not based on real security but on fear.

Even if you're apathetic, there is fear. It is a fear of expressing the rage that lies deep down inside. It is safer to feel dead. To feel the anger would mean doing something about it.

Underneath all of these fears is the fear of really facing yourself and developing your *me*. Once you understand the fear, you can begin to work on the problem. You can let go of your need to please and focus on yourself as a person.

FOCUS ON YOUR FEELINGS

Take some time to do the following exercise as a way of beginning to look deep inside and express your true feelings about yourself, your man and your relationship.

1. Write a letter to your mother describing all the details of your relationship. Remember this is only an exercise and you will not be mailing this letter, so you can be honest.

As you write, are you surprised at how much you have withheld? Or how subtly you have presented a false picture of your relationship?

2. When you have finished the letter, lay it aside, get out a picture of your mother and take a good look at it. Then try to put yourself inside her mind and reread the letter as though you were her. Are you surprised by what you read? Do you feel critical of your daugh-

ter? Do you feel sorry for her? Do you feel guilty because you were not a good role model?

3. Write a response to the letter as though your mother were writing it. Would she be easier on you than you are being on yourself? Would she understand how you got yourself into this kind of situation? Would she want you to leave or stay? Would she be angry that you couldn't make your relationship work?

Ask yourself how your grandmother would have reacted to your description of your relationship and the difficulties you are having.

As you think more about the letter you wrote and your mother's response, become aware of how much you wish to please her (even if she is no longer living) or how much you need to rebel against her lifestyle. Perhaps it is holding you back that she would be envious if you made a life for yourself like the one she wanted but never had. Could you live with that envy?

This exercise should begin to put you in touch with your true feelings about the relationship you're in— and some of your underlying reasons for staying. Once you have started this process, you may find that a dramatic change has to occur in your relationship . . . it's a matter of life and death for you. It may even mean that you'll have to leave your man in order to save yourself.

In the next chapter we'll look at what happens when women who are trapped in subservient, pleasing behavior finally reach a breaking point.

8

THE BREAKING
POINT

He complained about the dinner after that, and asked her why she didn't cook something he could eat, and he stormed out of the house afterwards, furious, supposedly to play tennis with a friend while it was still light, but she suspected that he was doing something else. He smelled even boozier when he got back and he wasn't wearing his tennis clothes. There were times when Jane even wondered if he cheated on her, hard as that seemed to believe, given what he did to her sexually. But he didn't lay a hand on her, he just berated her again for the damage she had done to the car, and called her a "dumb cunt," and *as he said those words she could feel something snap inside.* She had taken enough abuse over the years, and the truth was that that was what he thought of her. He thought of her as a piece of meat he had bought years before and could use as he chose.

—*Secrets,* by Danielle Steel
(Dell, 1985)

In this story, Jane had been living with her controlling man for many years and she'd rarely confronted him directly about his behavior. Secretly she fulfilled her own needs by pursuing a career as a supporting actress in a soap opera—he knew nothing about it. But now she had been offered a bigger part in a prime-time television series and she wanted it so badly that she had told him about it, even though she knew he would become even more abusive. The above incident took place shortly after she'd told him she was going to take the television role. Since he needed her to be passive and dependent upon him, this new threat did indeed push him into more abusive behavior. This abuse, coupled with the new confidence Jane felt about being approached for the television series, caused her to reach a breaking point.

For years, Jane had been weighing the pros and cons of this relationship. But the trade-offs—the children, their beautiful home, his sometimes charming behavior, the fear of being on her own—made it seem worthwhile to stay.

The story is familiar, although the abuse may not be as dramatic nor the stakes (a starring TV role) as tempting. I know a woman who gave one afternoon a week as a hospital volunteer. She enjoyed it and was about to earn a gold pin for fifty hours of service. But her husband became so critical about her being away from home, she quit just to have peace in the house. It made her very resentful to be pressured to give up something she cared so much about. When the breaking point is reached, things have probably been bad for a long time, and there have probably been many failed attempts at negotiation. Then something changes. Maybe you have reason to feel more confidence—you get a job promotion, for example. Or, for some reason, you feel less dependent on being in the relationship . . . and, at that point, he does something that strikes you as *the last straw*. Step seven in your recovery is recognizing that critical moment.

The breaking point. It is the point when you know it is over, and it usually comes in a blinding flash of realization. It is a powerfully moving experience, and, although you may not necessarily act at that moment, you don't forget it.

I have talked with many women about their breaking points, and all of them clearly recognized that dramatic point of no return. Here is what some of these women said:

- "I was stretched out sunning myself on the beach, and I thought I looked pretty good in my bikini. He glanced over at some teenage girls and said, 'I bet you looked that good when you were young.' "— Sandy, twenty-six-year-old model.
- "I got up in the middle of the night because I heard noises and tiptoed into the living room. There on the floor was my husband, having sex with my best friend and neighbor. I knew that was it."

- "It was when my daughter, at age thirteen, told me that her daddy had fooled around with her. I could never look in his eyes again."

- "You're not going to believe this, but it was an unpaid parking ticket that did it. He had been so irresponsible for so long that this was just the last straw."

- "He called from the police station saying that he had been arrested for drunk driving again. I went down and bailed him out. As we drove home, while he was talking about how he was innocent and had been framed, I was planning when I was going to leave."

- "The postman happened to mention that my husband had rented a box at the post office. I knew without asking that it was how he was carrying on an affair he had promised me was over. I turned icy cold inside."

- "He was watching TV in a T-shirt on New Year's Eve day and I was vacuuming the house for a visit from his mother. He told me to get him a glass of ice tea . . . and he said it like an order. After years of waiting on him without question, I said, 'Get it yourself.' And went to call a lawyer."

When it comes, the breaking point does not involve a rational decision based on years of weighing the pros and cons. It is more like a final blow, a sudden startling awareness of the way your self-esteem has been compromised . . . *a deep acknowledgment of the hurt that has been there time and again . . . a humiliation that cuts to the core . . . an inconsolable grief*

*over the loss of everything that has been of value in
your life.*

Kathleen, a woman I saw in my practice, related
this story to me:

"I had been divorced for five years when I met
Larry. We had an instant attraction and I was
thrilled. Everything seemed perfect—we shared all
the same interests and we had a wonderful time together. One of the things that I really liked about
Larry was how he doted on me—he called me three
times a day and I was used to men who promised to
call and never did. Larry made me feel special with
his attention. And I was flattered because he was a
very handsome and charming guy with lots of friends,
and I liked the idea that his friends could see that he
had chosen me.

"Larry drank a lot, but I didn't notice there was a
problem until I knew him for awhile. Even then, I
didn't really care because Larry got so sweet and
sentimental when he was drinking. No man had ever
talked to me that way before—he was so incredibly
romantic.

"Eventually, though, his behavior became very er-
ratic when he drank. Sometimes he would fly into a
rage over nothing—once he hit me. By this time, I was
really hooked on him and I thought maybe I could
help him become normal again.

"This went on for two years and things got increasingly bad but, for some reason, I denied that there
was a serious problem. I really felt I loved him and
he loved me and nothing else mattered. We could
work out our problems. But there was always an underlying tension, a fear because I never really knew
what he would do.

"The breaking point came at a party. He got very drunk and he started coming on to this other woman. It was an automatic reaction for me to get him out of embarrassing drunken situations, so when I saw what was happening, I took his arm gently and said, 'Come on, Larry. It's time for us to go.' He jerked his arm away with great force and shouted, 'How dare you tell me what to do!'

I didn't say anything—what was the point? He was drunk—and I walked away to the other side of the terrace and watched him locked in a passionate embrace with this woman. And suddenly something in me just snapped. Usually, when he treated me badly, my reaction was to cry and feel miserable, but I didn't cry. I felt completely empty of all feeling. I walked out and got a cab and I remember riding in the cab and having this cold, hard realization that I could no longer put up with it. And there was a tremendous relief, knowing that the abuse, the humiliation and the fights were over."

The incident that precipitates a breaking point is not always of dramatic proportions—sometimes it can be as mundane as that unpaid parking ticket. The feeling that something is terribly wrong often develops over a period of months or even years, a slow awakening to the truth. But the breaking point usually comes in an instant. The most common triggers are discoveries of a major indiscretion such as incest, an illegal act outside the home, an affair with a friend or relative, or physical abuse.

And usually, the stage has already been set, not by any action of the controlling man, but by two kinds of changes in *you* that allow you to see the abuse more clearly and to feel more strongly that you don't deserve it.

Increased self confidence: When you feel good about yourself, you are less likely to tolerate mistreatment. You feel that you deserve better. The same actions that you accepted when you had lower self-esteem now become unacceptable in the face of your sense of worth.

Often this confidence arises from a change in your financial situation. Janice, a forty-two-year-old lawyer, told me about her breaking point ten years ago. It was a dramatic eye-opening moment when she realized that she was going to leave her unhappy marriage.

Janice had started a business at home selling and installing window treatments, especially venetian blinds. She'd set up the business on her own, in spite of criticism and ridicule from her lawyer husband. She advertised and eventually built up such a large clientele that she had to move the business from her home into an office. Gradually she began to hire people to sell and install the products.

One afternoon as Janice sat doing her books, she was startled by the realization that she had made over $100,000. "It was a signal that I could go because I knew I could make it on my own." Two years later the couple parted amicably, and Janice started law school.

Another woman I spoke with inherited family money and felt that it gave her a way to finally leave her abusive husband. A third woman, at the age of fifty-four, left her husband when she found a live-in situation with a family in a nearby town, in which she could take care of their two-year-old. Leaving became feasible not only because she had a way of managing financially, but because it felt good to be needed.

Any situation that awakens you to your own self-worth is bound to create a crisis when you're with a controlling man. That's because the foundation of your relationship has been his power and your weakness. One woman confided that she gained self-confidence from having an affair with a man she met through work. "Suddenly I saw how he appreciated and respected me," she said. "And I compared his attitude with that of my husband. I said, 'Hey, I don't deserve this.' "

A loosening of ties: Perhaps the most common example of this is when the last child leaves for college. The reason for staying—because of the children—is no longer valid, and the family structure is weakened by the children's departure. Left alone in their empty nest, the partners begin to take a good look at each other and at their relationship for the first time in a long while. If things are bad, it is harder to make justifications.

The death of a child can also loosen ties. So can the end of responsibility for an extended family member, like an elderly parent.

Judith, aged thirty-two, described to me how involved she and her husband had been in helping his mother, who lived only a few blocks away. They had no children, but they jointly cared for his mother. Although she was unhappy in the relationship, Judith felt a deep sense of responsibility about this and wouldn't even consider leaving her husband. Finally the time came when they placed his mother in a nursing home, and this allowed Judith to take a hard look at her marriage. She left a year later.

As your confidence and independence begin to increase, there are fewer reasons to stay—the scales are tipped toward leaving. You begin to feel a little less frightened about looking at yourself. You have a new sense of freedom in the realization that you are responsible for yourself, and that it is not up to you to change him.

THE LAST STRAW

How did you arrive at that moment when you realized you had to either get out or assertively demand a radical change in your relationship? Was it a long, exhaustive struggle? A roller-coaster ride through good times and bad? A shocking revelation about him?

How you arrived at your breaking point has a lot to do with how much you will have to struggle to rebuild a life without your man. So too, do your age, values, support systems and other factors that will be discussed later in this chapter. By consciously evaluating your situation, you can determine whether, as a pleaser, you are at high or at low risk for having problems later on.

Every story about the deterioration of a relationship is unique and special. And yet there are generally four distinguishable patterns.

Exhaustion

"It's been bad for so long . . . I'm just tired of trying." This route to the breaking point is essentially a slow, downhill deterioration of the relationship. You have tried to make it work, but, near the end, your energy wanes and it seems useless to try anymore. None of the responses you've relied on—escape, passivity, and the others—works any longer. It's just hopeless.

Marci had been living with Paul for four years; during that time he promised repeatedly that they would be married, but he never came through. "Paul was a very glamorous guy. He worked in the film industry and he always had a lot of women around him. He told me not to worry about the others, he had chosen me, but at the same time he kept going back on his promise about getting married. And I knew that he sometimes went out with other women—he pretty much admitted that he had this 'problem' about women.

"Finally, I gave him an ultimatum and said that either he had to marry me or I was going to move out. He pleaded with me and said he just wasn't ready, but I held firm and moved into my own apartment. I didn't see him for two months, then he started calling and telling me how much he missed me and needed me. I finally agreed to see him. He begged me to come back and promised we'd work everything out this time. I agreed, but only after he promised to see a therapist to deal with his problems.

"I really thought everything was going to be okay. I was thrilled that Paul was seeing a therapist and I felt so optimistic about our future. He would go two nights a week, then come home and tell me how much it was helping him. Marriage seemed right around the corner.

"One night he came home from the therapist and I smelled liquor on his breath. I asked him where he had been and he said, 'At the therapist's.' I didn't believe him and I said, 'Oh, the therapist serves liquor?' Then he admitted that he hadn't gone to his appointment, but had been out at a bar with friends. I got angry because he had broken a very important promise. He got angry right back and told me that, in fact, he had *never* gone to the therapist. He'd just been pretending to appease me. I saw so clearly that nothing would ever change with him and if I didn't get out for good, I'd be stuck in the same situation until it was too late for me to have children. I left him that night—for good."

Shock

"How could this be happening . . . I thought we could work things out." In this pattern, you have used denial to handle your controlling man. But after awhile, that stops working and no longer protects you from the harshest truths. You wake up and see the pattern . . . or you are stunned by the evidence of one very disturbing event. This is the most devastating of all patterns because the breaking point hits you with little or no preparation.

"Things had been pretty rough for a long time," recalled Samantha in telling me about the shocking event that made her leave overnight. "Kyle was my second husband and I had three children from my first marriage. Sometimes I felt guilty because Kyle was so strict with the children, especially my son. Often he was downright mean.

"Kyle was German, and shortly after our marriage we moved to Frankfurt to live. It was a hard adjustment, but then I got a job teaching in an American army school and things started to settle down. I think I forgave Kyle a lot more than I should have because I knew he had been raised in a very harsh family environment. But I have to admit now that things were never really *good* between us.

"One night when Kyle was out of town on business, my eight-year-old son and I were sitting in the living room talking and I asked him if he liked Kyle. I was very concerned that my children be happy with this marriage. He said, 'Yes, I do. I like him.' So I asked, 'What do you like about him?'

"He pulled back then, and said, 'I can't tell you. It's a secret.'

"This made me *very* uncomfortable. There was something wrong here! I gently coaxed my son to tell me more and he finally said, 'We do secret things.'

"My heart nearly stopped beating. After some gentle prodding, I was able to win his confidence and he began to tell me about the sexual things Kyle did with him. Outwardly I remained calm, but my insides were churning with the horror of it. After my son went to sleep, I began to think about my daughters who were twelve and ten, and I went into their room and asked them point-blank if Kyle ever touched them. My eldest daughter said, 'When he reads to us at night, he gets into bed with us and I don't think he should do that.'

"I asked, 'Does he touch you?' And they both said yes. I left the room with the feeling that I just had to get the children away before Kyle came back from his trip. I called a friend and she came over that night to help me pack their things. At first I was just planning to send the children to my parents in California. I was going to stay and try to get help for Kyle. But in the midst of packing their things, I suddenly thought, 'Wait a minute! What am I thinking? I'm getting out, too.'

"We left and I never confronted him. In fact, I never saw or spoke to Kyle again. I began to build my life all over again. It was tough, but we're okay now."

Roller Coaster

"Our relationship has had its ups and downs . . . and it seems like there are a lot more downs lately." In this kind of relationship, the problems ebb and flow—sometimes it looks as though things are finally getting resolved, but then something else happens.

"The excitement was what attracted me to Joe in the first place," Vicki told me, describing her five-year marriage. "I had been raised in a very conservative family and Joe was different from any man I'd ever known. He was witty and charming and not afraid to take risks. Joe did everything to extremes. If he bought me flowers, it was always *three dozen* roses. When we went to a party, he was the last one to leave. He was wild and I loved that. It made me feel like a more interesting person myself to be around him.

"Even before we were married, I knew Joe saw

other women and drank too much, but I figured he would settle down some once we were married. I had this crazy idea that Joe could keep being an exciting person, but also be a family man at the same time. Of course it didn't happen that way. We had many terrible fights during our marriage about his drinking and his unreliability. And the fights began to take on a pattern. I would get very upset and start crying and go to the bedroom, and he would storm out of the apartment. Then later he'd come home with flowers or a gift and apologize to me and tell me he was going to try to be more responsible because he loved me and he couldn't bear to lose me. And he would get better for awhile—until the next time.

"The last straw for me was on a night we had a big dinner party. It was very successful and everyone had a good time. But Joe never knew when to quit and when everyone else was getting ready to go home, he was trying to talk people into going out to a club. Nobody wanted to do that, including me, and he was peeved and said he'd just go by himself. I went to bed.

"I woke up about three in the morning and the apartment was full of smoke. I ran into the living room and there was Joe, passed out on the couch. He had come home and fallen asleep smoking a cigarette. I dragged him up and we got out just before our entire living room went up in flames.

"We barely escaped with our lives and the apartment was completely destroyed. But it wasn't even that incident that really did it for me. It was the next day, when I found out that Joe hadn't paid the premium on the insurance and we had no coverage. It was just another example of his irresponsibility, but this time it was just too much for me to take."

Combination

"Sometimes I was exhausted from the tensions of subtle conflict with him . . . other times I was on a veritable roller coaster of ups and downs . . . and when we were up I was very much in love with him." In this pattern, the breaking point is usually reached after years of highs and lows—with some big shocks thrown in. Eventually, it all becomes too much and you walk away.

But no matter how you reached the breaking point, you're hurt, in shock, deeply angry and most certainly disoriented. It's not someone else's relationship that has broken up, after all. It's *yours*.

You wonder, "Will I survive? Will I ever be happy again?"

These thoughts and fears clutter your consciousness and make you feel weak and vulnerable. You are literally living in an identity vacuum—especially if all your energy during the relationship was focused on him. You look ahead and the future looms empty and frightening. You have no picture of what it's going to look like, but your greatest fear is that it will continue to look like a blank canvas.

Unfortunately there is no way to avoid these feelings. They must be faced, and the land mines of despair and defeat must be dealt with if you are to rebuild your life on a solid foundation.

Just as the paths to the breakup can vary, so too

can the paths to recovery. The length and severity of your rebound period depends on many different factors. And it's essentially a game of odds: the fewer debilitating factors, the better your chances for a speedy recovery.

REBOUND RISK POTENTIAL

How will you feel during the rebound period? Will you ease yourself through it slowly, minimizing the trauma? Or will you go to sleep each night wondering if you'll be able to get up the next morning?

Yes, it's tough to make this adjustment. But for some it's tougher than others. How can you predict what your own adjustment will be like?

I want to take you through an exercise in determining your risk potential. First, envision a continuum with "low risk" on one end and "high risk" on the other. I'll show you how to place yourself somewhere on the continuum.

HOW VULNERABLE ARE YOU?

1   2   3   4   5   6   7   8   9   10

LOW RISK   HIGH RISK

THE HIGH-RISK PROFILE

The odds are against Jenny having an easy time on
the rebound. She grew up in a small Wisconsin town,
the third of five children. She met Roger during her
first year of college. They dated for two years, then
married and moved to Boston.

Roger got his M.B.A. while Jenny worked as a typ-
ist to pay the bills. Once out of graduate school, Roger
began scaling the corporate ladder. Jenny stayed
home to raise their son and three daughters. With
time and Roger's success came a summer cottage on
Cape Cod and skiing trips at Christmas. As the children grew and went off to college, Jenny had more
time to travel with Roger on his business trips—and
they were a good team. He was the dashing, savvy
businessman and she was his elegantly dressed,
agreeable wife.

Life was easy and happy for Roger and Jenny . . .
until the night of their twenty-eighth wedding anni-
versary. They had just returned from a skiing trip
when Roger made his shocking confession: There
was another woman. He told Jenny that he wanted to
stay in the marriage but that she had to allow him to
see the other woman on occasion. Jenny couldn't
agree to those terms. She told him he would have to
leave.

Roger moved out several days later, leaving
Jenny in a state of collapse. What was she going to
do? How could she tell her parents? There had
never been a divorce in the family. Not only was it
against her upbringing, it was also against her religious convictions.

There was no one to turn to for help; her children

were away at school and she felt she couldn't burden her friends with her problems; they had their own. Besides, she was embarrassed to admit the truth. Hers had been the perfect marriage. Jenny cried and cried . . . and wondered what she had done wrong. Why had her marriage failed?

It's easy to see that Jenny is a high-risk candidate who is headed for big problems on the rebound.

— The end of her relationship came as a big shock to her; she had no time to prepare for it. It was not her decision.

— There is no history of divorce in her family, so hers is a unique experience, one for which she has yet to develop any problem-solving mechanisms.

— She was left by her husband . . . so she feels that she is somehow at fault for the divorce.

— Her entire life was centered around her husband and children, leaving her with little identity except that of wife and mother.

— She's fifty years old . . . and she feels she's past the point at which she can make a new life for herself.

— Her marriage lasted twenty-eight years, making a new life seem all the more impossible.

— Her traditional upbringing and religious convictions cause her to feel responsible and guilty for the divorce.

— Her dependency on her husband has left her unprepared to live on her own.

— With her children away at college, she may be suffering from the empty-nest syndrome. And simultaneously, she may be going through menopause.

Consider the following high-risk factors and evaluate how many of them are true for you.

High-Risk Factors

Vital Statistics

____ Shock-type ending to the relationship
____ First divorce
____ Middle-aged
____ Children
____ Relationship lasted more than ten years
____ Your man left you

Values and Experience

____ No history of divorce in your family
____ Traditional upbringing
____ Strong traditional religious convictions
____ Absent mother
____ Domineering father

Resources

____ Few financial resources
____ Lack of support (friends, relatives, therapy, etc.)
____ Poor physical health
____ Identity based on the relationship
____ Feeling that you are to blame for the breakup
____ Low self-esteem
____ Personality traits: naive, dependent, conforming, self-depreciating, eager to please, cynical
____ Simultaneous crises (addiction, illness, etc.)
____ Feeling that you need to conform to what is socially acceptable

If you find that these factors are not characteristic of your situation, consider yourself lucky. You may be more like Sue, whose story follows, than Jenny.

THE LOW-RISK PROFILE

Sue is a model of the woman with a low-risk potential. She is twenty-three years old and has been living with Rick for just over a year. She moved in with him rather than getting married because that's what he wanted. She was also worried about making the same mistake her divorced sister had.

Now things aren't working out. Rick doesn't trust her or give her enough freedom, and she's thinking about leaving. She knows she can go back to her parents for awhile, if she needs to, but she probably won't since she has a good job in computer technology. She's thinking about sharing an apartment with two friends she's known since grammar school.

Sue is at the low-risk end of the continuum.

— She has not been involved with Rick for very long.
— She is young, educated, and employed.
— She is the one who is leaving him.
— She is self-confident.
— There are no other crises to be handled at the same time.
— She has a strong support system.

You may be on the low-risk end of the continuum even if your situation is not exactly the same as Sue's. The following list of factors applies to low-risk rebound periods. But remember, even if the odds are in your favor, the rebound period is traumatic and needs to be negotiated carefully.

Low-Risk Factors

Vital Statistics

_____ Gradual dissolution of the relationship
_____ No marriage involved
_____ Under thirty years old
_____ No children
_____ The relationship lasted less than five years

Values and Experience

_____ History of successfully negotiated divorces in your family
_____ Non-traditional upbringing
_____ Influential religious convictions that don't make you feel guilty
_____ Strong female role models

Resources

_____ Adequate financial resources
_____ Emotional support from friends, relatives, therapy, etc.
_____ Good physical health
_____ Identity based on individual accomplishments
_____ Mind-set that your breakup was a "relationship that didn't work out"
_____ High self-esteem
_____ Personality traits: flexible, mature, worldly, hopeful, individualistic, assertive

_____ The breakup is the only crisis you are coping
with at this time

_____ No great need to feel socially acceptable

Just a word of general advice: no matter what your
situation, you should think of your breaking point as
a crisis. I like the way the Chinese define that word.
The two characters they use to make up *crisis* mean
"danger" and "opportunity." Yes, it is a dangerous
time . . . but it is also a time of opportunity for you.
The new situation you are being forced to face will
stretch your capabilities and increase your coping
mechanisms.

What is the real meaning of the high- and low-risk
continuums? How will your answers affect the way
you're most likely to operate in the world after you've
reached the breaking point?

The more items you checked on the high-risk lists,
the more likely you are to have a difficult time adjust-
ing after a breakup—even if the breakup was *your*
idea—and the more likely you are to seek "pseudo-
resolutions" rather than real resolutions. In the next
chapter we will discuss what these pseudo-resolu-
tions are and how easy it is for the woman with Me
Phobia to fall right back into the same traps that got
her into trouble in the first place.

9

FALSE SOLUTIONS
TO ME PHOBIA

You have now completed six of the eight steps in the recovery process from Me Phobia. At this point you probably have a pretty good intellectual understanding of your situation—why you are a pleaser and why you tend to get involved with men who are controlling.

What lies ahead may be a bit tougher because it calls for you to actually consider how you will make important changes in your behavior. But before we go forward, let's review the steps you have completed and why each one has been essential to your recovery process.

9

THE STEPS TO RECOVERY

So far in this book, you have completed the first six steps to recovery from Me Phobia. These are:

1. You recognized your Me Phobia and learned why it wouldn't work to satisfy your needs.
2. You pledged that you would go through all the steps in the recovery process.
3. You learned how men control you and how you respond to that control from the mind-set of the pleaser.
4. You identified how you became a pleaser and what factors are at the root of your Me Phobia.
5. You familiarized yourself with the typical stages in a relationship between a controlling man and a compliant woman.
6. You learned why you stay in your relationship even when it makes you unhappy—and how you come eventually to reach a breaking point.

The last three chapters will help you in the final and most critical stages of your recovery. These stages are:

7. Becoming aware of your tendency to seek false solutions to your relationship problems, being able to recognize the traps that lie ahead.
8. Finally, becoming a full and self-sufficient person—with or without a man.

Before you could even begin the process of recovery, you had to first recognize yourself as a woman with Me Phobia. You can't work on a problem that

you don't know you have. In the first step, you also
grew to understand why being submissive, compliant
and pleasing doesn't work to get the love and security
you desire. It only draws you to a certain kind of man,
a man you will never be able to please.

You now understand that as long as you live to
please, you will be attracted to men who appear to be
strong and who seem to want to take care of you. But
because they are also insecure and afraid of intimacy, they will only want to be with you as long as
they can control you. Locked into relationships with
these men, you will find that they are never able to
appreciate you for trying to please them, because that
would mean forfeiting their control. They are more
interested in controlling you than they are in loving
you.

This understanding should be a compelling enough
reason for you to want to change. No person wants
to be unhappy, and as a pleaser in a relationship with
a controlling man, you will never feel happy or secure. You live in a state of fear of making a mistake
that will bring criticism and displeasure. You will
never achieve true intimacy with your man.

Taking the first step and understanding why pleasing doesn't work probably motivated you to sign the
pledge at the end of Chapter One, promising yourself
that you were dedicated to making a change. This
pledge, which is step two in your recovery, is very
important; I'd like you to go back now to page 29 and
read it again. Consider how you feel now, compared
with how you felt when you signed it. You were probably leery then about whether or not you could do
what was necessary to change. Maybe you weren't
even sure that you needed to change. At that point,

you had no idea what conquering Me Phobia would entail. But you did make a promise that you would complete all the steps, and that is important. Pleasers are usually hard on themselves; many are perfectionists. You pride yourself in keeping the promises you make, so I know you took the pledge seriously when you signed it. If you *didn't* sign it then, thinking, "This is silly," do it right now. Unless you are willing to commit to the entire recovery process, you will not be able to go through the tough part ahead—the part where you will actually have to change your behavior.

In the third step I asked you to examine just how controlling the man or men in your life have been. It is important to your recovery to be able to identify the behaviors that bring you so much unhappiness. You can see now how a man can control you just as easily by using charm or protection as he can by abusing you or threatening to abuse you.

If you are playing relationship roulette with a controlling man, you must also understand *your* moves; the behavior you use to protect yourself from the dangers you instinctively feel from trying to please a controlling man. The second part of step three in your recovery involved becoming aware of the part you have played in the process that keeps you so unhappy. Remember, you originally gave him the doormat to step on. You consistently sent him the signals that you would continue to play the pleasing game. You never said, "No!" or "That's enough!" (and meant it). You became tolerant of behavior that at one time you would never have accepted. You became increasingly anxious to please him as you became more unhappy and the stakes became higher.

Maybe before you completed step three, you didn't realize how you played right into his hands—but now you know. Have you become the person you never thought you would become—bitchy, depressed, resentful, anxious? Whether you have tried to live your true life behind his back, have conned him to make the best of a bad situation, have thrown in the towel at times, or have exploded into brief fits of rage, you have still allowed him to control your reactions. He has seen that you are frustrated, angry, maybe even depressed to the point of being suicidal, but you are staying with him and still seem to want to make the relationship work. To him that means he has you where he wants you.

You now know that to recover from Me Phobia you can *no longer tolerate* controlling, overbearing behavior. You see that you are engaged in a hopeless struggle that will not lead to happiness or fulfillment in a relationship where both partners are equal.

Knowing that, you may have a tendency to say, "Okay, you're right. This is bad and I am playing a role in it. Therefore I must be bad or a loser." You cannot recover from Me Phobia if you fall into the self-blame trap. As a pleaser, you probably have never really felt good about yourself, deep down. And you need to develop a positive way of thinking about yourself: "I am important. I have rights. I deserve happiness." Yes, the situation has been bad and has no future. Yes, you are playing a role in the mess. But as you learned in step four, your conditioning had a lot to do with your trying always to win approval by pleasing. Go easy on yourself, because not only are you not to blame for the way you were conditioned, but you are in good company—most women had exactly the same kind of conditioning.

In step five you learned about the typical stages of a relationship between a controlling man and a pleasing woman. You saw the initial thrill and ultimate futility of such relationships, and this probably motivated you further to get rid of your Me Phobia so you could have a fulfilling relationship with a man.

If, as you read this book, you are at the beginning of a relationship that has all the hallmarks described here, perhaps it is early enough to make a clean break and refuse to let your man assume a controlling position in your life. If you are midway through a relationship with a controlling man, you can now see what lies ahead. You are the judge about whether or not you should put a stop to the miserable cycle. If your relationship seems near the end (according to the description of the stages), you can take comfort in now knowing that it could never have turned out any differently. You did your best in light of what you had to give and who you have been as a person. This step is particularly important if you are a pleaser who has been at the negotiating stage repeatedly and still find yourself stuck in a relationship that never really gets better.

If you have felt stuck in this way, you learned in step six why a woman like yourself might stay in a relationship even when it has become intolerable. And you listened to many women tell the stories of what finally caused them to reach a breaking point. Step six also gave you guidelines that allowed you to evaluate what your risk potential is for problems if you should decide to leave the relationship.

Having completed the first six steps of the recovery program, you may think that you don't really need to finish the process. You are probably feeling stronger now that you understand the problem, and maybe you are confident that you know what to do.

But if you only go this far, without completing the exercises in chapter nine, you are setting yourself up to fall into traps I call "pseudo-solutions" to the problem of Me Phobia. Let me warn you in advance. It is easy to seek shortcuts at this point and never allow yourself to get to the bottom of your Me Phobia. These shortcuts (such as entering a new relationship with the same kind of man) will only put you right back into the same state you're currently in.

Now you're ready for step seven, where we'll look at some of the false solutions you need to be wary of as you continue your recovery process.

TRADING IN YOUR MAN

When you are miserable enough in a relationship that you have reached a breaking point, it is natural to feel bitter. This man, who once was the object of your love and devotion, has turned into the enemy. Your thoughts turn to visions of the perfect mate, a man who seems to have none of the bad qualities you now associate with the one who caused you so much anguish. Your mind might be flashing back to other men you knew before you were involved with him. You think, "What if?" Rather than looking inside yourself to better understand your true needs and desires, you rush out to trade in your man for a different and better model. The focus of your attention is once more on *him,* not on yourself.

Marcia ended her marriage when it became unbearable, but still anxious to please, she immediately entered into a new relationship. For two years now she has been married to a man who is very different from her first husband. George is the strong, silent type, a good provider and a responsible partner. But whenever Marcia tries to talk to him about anything concerning her feelings, he blows up at her. If she pursues the point, his temper tantrum freezes into a silent treatment that sometimes last as long as two or three weeks.

Marcia is confused. How can she be so unhappy when she has married a man who is completely the opposite of her first husband? "He was a total mess-up," she recalls. "A two-timer. Sometimes he'd just pick up and leave me and the kids for weeks with no money. And it was just as bad when he was home ... he slapped me around a lot when he drank."

Deep down inside, Marcia believes she should be grateful to her new husband, for providing her with a stable existence. She feels guilty about her unhappiness with him, but wonders if she has made another wrong choice on the opposite end of the spectrum.

The truth is that Marcia is not capable of making the right choice until she makes some changes in herself. If she continues the way she is going, she might eventually divorce her second husband and try again, this time improving her situation a little. Again, she would feel lucky for awhile but gradually begin to realize that something was still wrong. Marcia needs to hear the message loud and clear—*it is her problem, her need to please, her bad case of Me Phobia* that is attracting her again and again to controlling men.

Marcia has been "trading up" in her relationships with men. Another pseudo-solution is "trading around." In this scenario, you haven't confronted the problem of pleasing that lies within yourself. Rather, you think the men you have chosen are too weak or too strong, too successful or too much of a failure, too old or too young, too competitive or not competitive enough.

Nancy married young and married well. Or so she thought. Alan was rich and very successful. He courted her with furs, expensive cars, and trips to exotic places. Nancy was thrilled. Alan was surely the best thing that had happened in her life, and he came along at just the right time to lift her out of the terrible gloom caused by her mother's death in an automobile accident.

They were married three months after they met. Once they were married, things began to change. Alan was obsessively jealous, following Nancy to her classes at the local college and listening in on her phone calls. Nothing she did could please him. Then he began hitting her as punishment for her alleged crimes. Nancy's father rescued her and took her home.

A year later she met Jason. He was a gentle, sensitive man who earned a meager living writing magazine articles. He moved into the apartment Nancy's father had set her up in after her first marriage. Nancy gave Jason a lot of attention and even financed their living expenses so he could get on his feet. She took care of all his needs, but as she said later, "He could never perform." Eventually, she asked him to move out.

Now she is involved with a man ten years her junior who is very successful. She thinks this might be the right combination of characteristics—young enough not to be overbearing, but successful rather than weak.

The problem is that Nancy is still Me Phobic. The men she chooses may be different in many ways, but they all treat her like the little girl she evidently still wants to be. They overpower her, or protect her too much, or are too weak to take care of her. Nothing will be right for Nancy until she learns to relate to the men in her life as a mature woman and view herself as their equal.

You might even "trade down" and choose a man who is vastly inferior to you in looks, social standing, intelligence, or income. Your logic is that a man who feels inferior to you will feel lucky to have you and will never leave. Finally you can feel loved and secure.

This man is often inferior to the controlling man you have left. When Melissa left Frank, she was determined that she would never again fall for a corporate type. Frank was very self-assured and successful, and Melissa believed that he controlled her because he was in a position of such natural authority. After she left Frank, she entered into a number of affairs with "bad boys"—married men, unemployed men, men involved with drugs. These relationships were all initially exciting and ultimately traumatic, but Melissa was hooked on the good feelings she had when she helped the bad boys. Once she lent money to her boyfriend, a cocaine addict who told her straight out that he needed the money to buy drugs. Melissa knew this was the wrong thing to do, but she comforted herself with the thought that he needed her and would stay with her as long as she could help him.

MAKING MEN THE BAD GUYS

Another pseudo-solution is deciding that men are no good, blaming them for all your troubles. After ending a relationship with a controlling man you might say, "I'm not going to let men use and abuse me . . . I can play that game, too." I have talked to many young women who frequent singles bars, and I've found that this is a common way of thinking for them. These women openly seduce men, get them hooked either with or without sex, and then cruelly reject them. Their feeling of satisfaction is fleeting and maybe it makes up a bit for the hurt they experienced in past relationships. But this attitude does little to prepare them for true intimacy with a man. Some women decide to live completely without men, and this only leads to unhappiness and bitterness.

Don't get me wrong: of course you can live a normal, fulfilling life even if you don't have a man around the house. But if you make that decision because of resentment, it is not a healthy resolution. It is certainly not dealing with your Me Phobia, because you are still *reacting to* men. In this case, you are letting your bitterness against them control your life.

Frances came to see me in my practice because she was experiencing depression. "I'm so tired lately," she told me. "I have trouble sleeping and eating and I feel generally lethargic. My doctor says there's nothing physically wrong . . . so here I am."

I questioned her about her job, her family, and her living situation. Frances was a magazine editor, and she confessed that she frequently put in as many as fifteen hours a day, even on the weekends.

"You might be feeling burned-out from so much pressure at work," I suggested. "It sounds like you take very little time to relax—you don't recover from one day's work before you're back in the thick of it again."

I asked Frances about her relationships, and she grimaced. "That's one worry I don't have, thank God."

"What do you mean?"

"I was much worse off when I was living with Paul," she said. "Now *that* was stress! He made my life miserable with his drinking and womanizing. I couldn't even concentrate on my job. I'm better off without him. In fact," she said, "it seems that every time I get involved with a man, it screws up my life. I just can't take that pressure anymore."

Frances had convinced herself that men were the problem in her life, and she tried to solve this by throwing herself completely into her work. She didn't understand why she still felt so unhappy. I suspected that it was because she had never resolved her bitterness, and had closed off the possibility of finding the true love and intimacy that she still desired. Frances was an angry woman who was very much controlled by men, even as she rejected them.

THE REBOUND SYNDROME

We've all heard the warning, "Watch out, you're on the rebound." And in fact, there is a tendency when one relationship has ended to simply bounce into another one, using the narcotic of being in love to numb you to the real task that lies ahead in your development. Compulsive dating and sleeping around is often an unconscious effort to skip the stage at which you sort things out for yourself, the stage where you finally have the time and the space to do the necessary work of confronting your Me Phobia. When you do this, you are truly, as the song says, "Looking for love in all the wrong places." Your time alone after a divorce or breakup can be used to get to know yourself and learn to like yourself. It is a precious commodity—not one to be wasted on throwing yourself at new relationships.

Lois was angry when she broke up with Byron—angry that she had "wasted" so many years on him. She was thirty-five years old and she had lived with Byron for eight years, finally leaving him when she became convinced that he would never marry her and give her the children she wanted so desperately. Within six months after leaving Byron, Lois was married. Shortly after that, she was pregnant. Her excitement with the pregnancy covered up the fact that Lois didn't love her husband; she wasn't really happy in the relationship. Women like Lois may find what they want in the short term, but in the long run they are doomed to frustration and misery.

I understand that many women in their thirties are panic-stricken by the biological clock and they fall into bad relationships because they want so much to have children. But this is a weak foundation on which to build a lifetime of intimacy. Indeed, some women end up resenting the children because their conception pushed them to marry the wrong man.

LIVING IN THE PAST

Maybe you have left the relationship but you haven't completely gotten over it. Deep down, you still believe that if you try to mold yourself into someone he would like—if you are good enough, bright enough, interesting enough, or self sufficient enough—he might take you back. I know a woman who lost thirty pounds and developed a new glamorous look, then arranged to be at a party where she knew she'd run into her ex-husband. She wanted him to feel as if he were really missing out by not having her, this newly exciting and beautiful woman. She was still stuck in an effort to please him. When he paid no attention to her at all, this sent her into new waves of despair and caused her to overeat, gaining back all the weight she had lost.

Another woman I spoke with had an affair with an old boyfriend after her marriage broke up. This was a man she had lived with several years before she got married. She had left him because of his drinking, and he was still drinking when she went back to him. But she had managed to convince herself that he wasn't so bad after all. There was some security in choosing a man she already knew, rather than doing the hard work required to build a brand new life for herself. Of course, this relationship failed for the same reasons it had the first time, leaving her even more miserable and insecure.

SEEKING AN AUTHORITY

Another pseudo-solution is to join a group in which an authority does the thinking and your behavior is rigidly monitored. These groups, whether religious, political, or a form of psychological therapy, can be repressive because they encourage dependency. Locked into a ready-made worldview, you never get a chance to really explore who you are. It is easy to be sucked into these groups, because they reward those who love to please. The signals are very clear— perhaps the clearest you've ever had. You know exactly what to say and think, and how to act to be approved of. And you have the added benefit of feeling that you're growing while you do it.

The truth is, you are simply engaged in a parallel rerun of your relationship to a controlling man—only now you are married to a controlling group.

COMPULSIVE BEHAVIOR

Any kind of compulsive behavior can be used to blunt the anxiety of having to face yourself, but in the end it will make you feel worse, not better.

How can you feel good about yourself if you need, for example, to buy a new dress or a pair of shoes in order to experience yourself as a valuable person? Compulsive buying, compulsive eating, compulsive drinking and compulsive cleaning are all pseudo-solutions that don't work. They trick you into thinking that you are making yourself feel better, but they ultimately undermine your confidence. Even compulsive exercising can be detrimental, although taking good care of your body is, as you will see in the next chapter, one of the most important aspects of your recovery from Me Phobia.

I know a woman who became obsessed with doing aerobics. Initially she joined a class to get into shape. And she became hooked on the good feelings the exercise caused. Soon she was going to classes three times a day—before work, during lunch, and in the evening. All her free time was devoted to exercising. Not only was this unhealthy (eventually she stopped menstruating and experienced other physical problems), it also controlled all of her time and mental resources. It was just another form of escape from herself.

Face it. Shopping, cleaning, or exercising are, in and of themselves, too simplistic to be real, effective ways of dealing with a problem as serious as Me Phobia. Yes, it's important to buy nice things for yourself. Yes, it's important to live in a neat and attractive environment. Yes, it's important to look good and have a healthy body. But when these become the center of your existence, you know that you have stumbled on a pseudo-solution to your Me Phobia.

FINDING THE REAL SOLUTION

The *real* solutions—those that will lead you to self-discovery—are harder to come by. But they're worth the hard work.

You have already taken many of the steps necessary to prepare yourself for the last big one—the one that requires you to make real changes in your behavior. In the next chapter you will be asked to complete exercises that may be uncomfortable for you. Some will be harder than others. Don't worry about whether you are completing them in the right order or in the right way. You don't have to worry about pleasing anyone! You will know deep in your heart if you are really giving the program a chance and how hard you are trying.

The key factor will be *practice,* a simple idea, and one that you probably associate with learning to play the piano as a child or learning to type as a teenager. Practice is something we have to do all our lives, every time we're confronted with something new.

Overcoming your fear of the unknown is not something that happens through understanding alone. You probably already know that. You may have *understood* for some time that you were trapped in a cycle of pleasing men, but you did not know how else to behave or how to change.

Getting to know yourself is something you must practice as a part of a regular routine. And you will never be finished with the process because, as a person, you will always be changing. Just as golf professionals still practice before every round, so you will have to continue practicing, even after you become a pro at getting to know yourself.

10

FACING ME

When it came time to write this chapter, I took a week off from my responsibilities and rented a room in a motel near the beach on Long Island. I took my typewriter, papers, and some books, and planned to stay there alone for four days and three nights.

I felt very excited, because it was the first time I had been away by myself for a long while; I could take care of *me* and not have to worry about other people's expectations.

When I arrived, I went to the supermarket to shop and delighted in the idea that I could buy anything I wanted—I didn't have to worry, as I normally did, about someone else. I found, too, that I enjoyed the luxury of cooking, when just days before I had been complaining to my husband about how much of a burden it had become. The days fell into a kind of

structure, with two-hour typing stretches inter-
spersed with walks on the beach or drives to nearby
towns.

On the evening of the second day, I got lonely and
called my husband. I wondered if he could possibly
get away, and make the three-hour drive to come for
dinner and stay overnight. As soon as he said he
couldn't rearrange his schedule, I was glad. I started
on my project with a renewed vigor, and I found that
my initial excitement about being away had shifted
to a mood of serenity.

I talked to myself a lot and listened more carefully
to my inner voices. I ate when I was hungry and slept
when I was tired. It was the perfect setting for me to
put together my final ideas on recovering from Me
Phobia and to continue my own ongoing recovery
process. I felt that I was *living* the experience of what
I was writing. In that precious solitary environment,
away from the needs of others, I could be kind to
myself and listen to my own needs.

Once upon a time, a woman moved to a cave in
the mountains to study with a guru. She wanted,
she said, to learn everything there was to know.
The guru supplied her with stacks of books and left
her alone so she could study. Every morning the
guru returned to the cave to monitor her progress.
In his hand he carried a heavy wooden cane. Each
morning he asked her the same question: "Have
you learned everything there is to know yet?"
Every morning her answer was the same: "No, I
haven't." The guru would then strike her over the
head with his cane.

This scenario was repeated daily over a period

of months. One day the guru entered the cave,
asked the question, heard her answer and raised
his cane to hit her. But she grabbed the cane from
his hands, stopping the assault.

The woman looked up at the guru. She was relieved that the daily batterings were over, but she
feared reprisal. To her surprise, he smiled. "Con-
gratulations," he said. "You have graduated. You
now know everything you need to know."

"How's that?" the woman asked.

"You have learned that you will never learn
everything there is to know," he replied. "And you
have learned how to stop the pain."

Told by Scott Egleston to Melody Beattie and
published in her book *Codependent No More;*
Harper/Hazeldon, 1987.

You are now ready to take the final step in stopping
the pain of living as a Me Phobic—someone who has
an irrational fear of looking at herself and getting to
know herself; someone who doesn't know what it
means to honor herself; someone who defines herself
by and through the approval of others, most especially by a controlling man.

You are now ready for the most important and the
most difficult part of the recovery process. It is also
the most exciting and the most rewarding part.

I want to stress that, in taking step eight, you will
not be developing a self as much as you will be getting to know who you already are. Once you take a
good look inside, you may or may not like what you
find. You may even *want* to change something. That's
up to you. What I'm doing here is helping you to take

that inward look by showing you ways that you can hold that mirror up to yourself.

As you proceed, you may become anxious about what you are doing. In fact, you may even try in some way to sabotage the process. You might decide that this is all silly. Or you may get bored with the exercises and stop doing them. Or you may feel pressured by responsibilities at work or at home, and lay the book aside for awhile. Just remember that these responses are signs of your anxiety. You are frightened of looking at yourself—that is your affliction.

Your recovery from Me Phobia, however, is predicated on your fulfillment of the pledge you signed in the second step of the process—to complete all the steps. So I urge you to press ahead, even if the going gets rough at times.

It's important that you know that you *can* do things you feel fearful about. You don't have to be perfectly comfortable in order to begin one of these exercises. Just start and handle your fears as you go. It might make it easier for you to establish the order in which you do the exercises. As long as you do them all eventually, you will have completed the last step in your recovery. If it's easier, do them one or two at a time. Buy a loose-leaf notebook for your assignments, and write the name of each one at the top of a blank page.

Besides buying a notebook, it is important to tell the special people in your life that you are going to take this time to figure out who you are. That's right, tell them: the man in your life, your children, if they are old enough, your good friends. They all need to know that you're up to something new. Telling others is probably something you're reluctant to do. You might have thought you could do this work behind closed doors, because if nobody knows what you're doing, no one has to know if you fail. You're probably also afraid that others will put you down or criticize you for taking on this task.

Let's proceed, though, with confidence that you will *succeed,* completing all the exercises and ending up being much more in touch with yourself. That will mean changes in your behavior. And while you can't warn your loved ones about any specific changes (you don't know yet what they'll be!), at least you can let them know that change is in the air.

Be prepared for some condescending remarks, especially from your controlling man, when you tell him what you are about to do. Change is very threatening to this kind of man, particularly change over which he has no control. You may even find that his controlling behavior will escalate or that he will add one or two new maneuvers to his repertoire. Don't let his response get you off-track. Don't let him frighten you.

If you find that you are too frightened of him to even begin step eight, you should stop right here and get professional counseling. You need much more than I can give you through the written word. You need support and encouragement to take a good long look at your fears and your options.

Besides buying a loose-leaf notebook for your assignments and preparing those close to you for your adventure, there is a third thing you should do before you begin. Try to find another woman to work on these exercises with you. That may be difficult and you may be embarrassed about approaching someone to play the buddy role, but you will be better off in the long run. Choose someone to do the exercises with you, or someone to whom you can report about your progress. It can make a difference to have a friend who will be pleased by your adventure—you can definitely use that positive support in completing the final step.

FACING ME

"If you want to really understand something, try to change it."

I heard this statement years ago, and I believe it is completely true. It is the perfect context in which to begin step eight of your recovery, and in which to do these exercises that will make an important change in your life.

1. Choose a New Direction

Go back to a time in your life when you were at an important crossroad. Perhaps it was the time just before you got married or just before you got your first full-time job. Maybe it was when you moved out of your parents' house.

Use your notebook to record the following reflections:

— Identify the crossroad.
— Describe the road you took and why.
— Describe the road(s) not taken and why.
— Develop further what your life would have been like had you taken one of the other roads.

— What appeals to you now about the other life you
  chose not to live?
— What frightens you about it?
— Is there any element of that untraveled road that
  you can now put into your life?

A friend of mine, after doing this exercise, remembered that she had wanted to be an anthropologist
before her parents talked her into going to nursing
school. She decided to join Earth Watch, an organiza-
tion that sponsors archeological digs and stimulates
lay interest in the field.

This exercise will help you tune into past aspects
of yourself that might have become lost or overshadowed by your need to please.

2. Be Your Own Good Mother

Ask yourself *three times* during the course of every
day: "How am I doing?" Monitor your feelings. Try to
describe how you are really feeling and what practical things you would need to do to make yourself feel
better. Imagine having a fairy godmother, the epitome
of a good mother, who would meet those needs. Then
do one thing for yourself that a good mother would do
if she were actually present.

Below is a sample of a business-size card I developed for a group of women lawyers in New York. Cut
it out or make one of your own and carry it with you
in your wallet. It will remind you of the areas you
should ask yourself about when you monitor your
feelings.

HOW AM I DOING?

* Emotionally?   * Nutritionally?

* Financially?   * Intellectually?

* Spiritually?   * Professionally?

* Physically?   * Culturally?

* Sexually?

---

3. Name Your Feelings

If you had trouble doing exercise number two, it may be because you have lost touch with the way you feel. You may even have forgotten the possible range of human feelings you have to choose from in your description of how you are doing. Try this exercise, then go back to number two—it will be easier.

— Write down as many feelings as you can think of (anger, sadness, jealousy, excitement, joy, grief, boredom, fear, resentment, etc.).
— From magazines or newspapers, cut out pictures of people's faces that reflect each of these feelings. Glue the pictures on a sheet of notebook paper and label each face with the corresponding feeling.
— Practice identifying the feelings of others as you interact with them in your daily life or as you watch them on television. Record these in your

notebook. For example, you might write, "Mary Lou was feeling sad today . . ."

4. Find a Cause

The goal here is to publicly identify yourself with a cause or an issue so you can find out how it feels to have a strong opinion, and learn how to defend yourself against people who will be critical of your stand.

— Read your local newspaper and think about what is happening in your community—the issues that are being addressed and the things that need to be done.
— Choose an area that interests you and that you believe in. It doesn't have to be controversial.
— Volunteer to do something for that cause.
— Wear a button in public supporting that cause. If buttons are not available, have one made. This is a crucial step—don't skip it! Defending your position on an issue will give you the practice you need to stand up to those who might not agree with you.

5. Pull In Your Antennae

With your extreme sensitivity to what others need from you, it is easy to get off the track of identifying your own feelings and opinions about people and situations. Try this trick:

— When you get confused about what you think, assume that there is someone around who is trying to influence you in his or her direction—perhaps to bully you.

— Identify who that person is.

— The next time you are with that person and he or she begins to talk, turn your body sideways so your stomach is not facing the person, and continue to look at him or her as you talk. (Practice this in front of a mirror so you can do it without appearing too awkward.)

— Cover your stomach with crossed arms in a casual gesture.

— Now, think about how you feel about what this person is saying. Are you better able to see that he or she has a right to an opinion but that you also have a right to yours?

This exercise is based on the premise that you feel the need to please *in your gut.* It's a primal reaction to fear. By protecting your gut from negative incoming stimuli, you are giving yourself more of a chance to hear what *you* are saying and feel what *you* are feeling.

6. Become a Novelist

Think of a plot that focuses on a woman much like yourself, but someone who has a life you would envy. Give your heroine a different name from yours and a different appearance. Now begin to write a description of her day-to-day life. Also write about her dreams for the future. You may want to spend several days on the construction of her life. (And, who knows, maybe it will turn into a full-length story or novel!)

When you have completed the story, do the following:

— Rewrite the story, changing the heroine's name to yours.
— Change her appearance to match yours.
— Write about the differences between your life and hers.
— Write about the similarities between your lives.
— Take one aspect of her life that you particularly envy and write down how you might make it a part of your life.

7. Create a Dream

If there is something you have always wanted to do but have considered it impossible, figure out a way to make it happen. For example, if you have always wanted to go up in a hot-air balloon, start a file about hot-air balloons. Collect clippings of stories about them, read books about them, try to talk to someone who has been up in one. Do anything you can think of that will involve you more in your dream. Finding a passion in your life that is something *you* care about (not just getting a new man or fixing your relationship) will go a long way toward making you feel more like the individual you are already becoming. And the more you engage yourself in this passion, the less impossible it will seem to you.

I know a woman who has a fascination with the

study of rocks and gems. Over the years she has read many books on the subject, but has never had the time or inclination to pursue her interest. She thought it was frivolous, and that her more serious duties should come first. But after doing this exercise, she delved into her interest, finding classes at a local college and even signing up for a rock-hunting excursion. "What I discovered," she says now, "is that my passion meant something important to me—yet all those years I had kept it hidden, as if I should be ashamed of loving something outside my family."

8. Talk to a Stranger

Seek out a stranger somewhere when you are away from your home turf (on an airplane, or sitting on a park bench in another town . . .). Once the conversation gets going, be on the lookout for opinions that he or she voices that are different from your own. Make a point of letting the stranger know that you disagree and why. If it gets too uncomfortable for you, you can always change the subject or leave. Don't try to be provocative—just give yourself the chance to state your opinions in an atmosphere where there is little to lose if the person decides that he or she doesn't like you.

If you feel that the other person is turning off to you or disapproving of what you say, experience it and tell yourself, "I guess it doesn't make any real difference what he thinks about me."

Try this exercise as many times as you need to until you no longer feel uncomfortable doing it.

9. Do Something Alone

Think about activities that people rarely pursue alone—going to a movie, eating out at a fancy restaurant or taking a vacation.

— Choose something to do alone.
— Concentrate on the pleasure of selecting something that you would enjoy. How does it feel not to have to take anyone else's preferences into account?
— Do nothing that will dilute the experience (like taking a book along to the fancy restaurant or sitting next to someone in the theater so people will think you're together). If you're sitting in a restaurant, be a people-watcher and involve yourself in thinking about *them,* rather than worrying about yourself.
— Imagine other people noticing you alone and admiring your courage.
— Later, write down how you felt about being alone in that situation—and include as many emotions as you felt (exhilaration, fear, pride, isolation, etc.).

10. Do Something New

Doing something for the first time, whether it be asking someone to put out a cigarette that is bothering you or working out on a Nautilus machine, gives you more confidence. You see that you can handle the unknown.

I remember the first time I had my boots shined by a bootblack on the streets of New York City. I decided that I wanted to try it one day when I noticed that I had never seen a woman availing herself of this service. After I made my decision to go ahead, I got nervous. For several days, wherever I walked, I noticed men getting their shoes shined. How much did it cost? How long would it take? How much should I tip? Finally, I summoned enough courage to do it. At first I felt nervous and embarrassed, but then I started to enjoy myself and feel proud. It was a small step but it changed the way I felt about myself. (And my boots looked great!)

This exercise will allow you to begin to experience new things. And it is one that you can do with a buddy, someone you can adventure with and celebrate with when you've accomplished something new—although I think it is even more exciting to face the unknown alone.

— Notice things that people are doing that you have never done. (It doesn't matter whether you are watching men or women.)
— Make a list of experiences you have never had and situations that you have never handled. This is a list that you should keep adding to.
— Once a month, choose one new thing that you decide to do.
— Later, write about the anxiety you felt while you were pursuing this new activity, or during the planning phase.
— After you've done it, detail your feelings. Note your sense of accomplishment, the high you get as you "invent" yourself.

It is important to keep a record in your loose-leaf notebook of each one of these first-time experiences. It will become a history of success that you can refer to on days when you feel you don't have the courage to continue to look at yourself.

Here are some examples of the kinds of first-time experiences you might consider:

— Talking to a homeless person.
— Telling a door-to-door salesman that you aren't interested in hearing his pitch and closing the door.
— Going out without a bra.
— Paying someone to help you around the house.
— Changing your hairstyle.
— Going to a dating service.
— Finding a place on the map where you have never been and driving there.

Now, you add to the list . . .

11. Break Your Typecast

Think about what type of person you are. If you are like most people, you have typecast yourself and you use certain words to describe yourself. You might say things like, "I am a shy person," or "I don't have a head for numbers." When you say these things about yourself, you believe that they really describe *you*. Not only does this kind of typecasting make you afraid to try new things, it also prevents you from experiencing new situations with a full range of emotions. For example, if you cast yourself as "tough," you don't allow yourself to be moved to tears by a touching movie.

This exercise will begin to free you to move beyond the role you have set for yourself.

— What ten words best describe you? (Use words like procrastinator, pleaser, pretty, unathletic, lazy, smart, tough, etc.)
— Read these ten words over and think about the preconceived notions you have about yourself.
— Which characteristics do you believe *really* describe you, and which have others told you reflect your personality? Trace each label back to its beginning.
— Which characteristics would you like to change? To what?

12. Imagine Your Success

Think about the ten most serious problems that you have on your mind right now. One might be how you are going to send your child to college next year when you are only squeaking by financially as it is. Another might be how to end the physical abuse from your man. Or how to lose the weight your doctor has recommended you take off.

— Write down each problem at the top of a separate sheet of paper.
— Brainstorm solutions for each problem and write down all your ideas.

— For each problem, choose one solution that, even though it might not seem entirely feasible, has the potential for solving the problem.
— Write a one-page scenario for each solution as though it worked. Describe your feelings upon discovering the answer and how your life feels now that this difficulty is out of the way.
— Now ask yourself: What can you realistically do in your own life about each of these problems?

The solutions you write down might lead you in the direction of real answers, but that's not the main purpose of this exercise. Rather the intention is to help you see how much you may be hiding behind your problems and using them as an excuse for not getting on with your life.

13. Control Your Worry Time

Make a section in your notebook that you will only use to worry about other people. Give yourself some time every day (no longer than fifteen or twenty minutes) to sit down and write about your concerns for your husband, children, parents, friends, neighbors. It is best not to give vent to these negative thoughts near bedtime because they stay in your consciousness and affect your level of confidence for the next day.

Promise yourself that at no other time of the day will you worry—you have this special time set aside to do your worrying.

This exercise has a number of purposes:

1. To allow you to see how much time you spend worrying about others.
2. To help you understand how much your concern for others interferes with your thinking about your own recovery from Me Phobia.
3. To enable you to see how ineffectual worrying is because it doesn't get down to real problem-solving—mostly it's just spinning wheels.
4. To give you an idea how much time and energy you would have for yourself if you would detach from others a bit and let them lead their own lives and be responsible for their own actions.

14. Strengthen Your Physical Self

Being in good physical shape, eating right and exercising will give you the extra energy you need to overcome your Me Phobia. The exercises you have completed so far will help build your psychological strength or self-confidence. But unless your body is honed for this adventure, you may not achieve the optimum results of recovery.

Conduct some physical tests to get to know your body better. The results will either pleasantly surprise you or convince you that you should do something about getting in shape.

— How many laps of a pool can you swim?
— How many blocks can you jog at a slow pace?
— How long can you run in place before your legs give out?
— How many stairs can you climb before you get winded?

— How many miles can you comfortably walk at a
  brisk pace?

You ask the questions and look at the answers. Get
to know your physical self and set some goals, if they
are needed, to get into better shape.

15. Know Your Disowned Self

Each one of us has many parts that make up the total
self. There is the part that wants to be taken care of,
the part that wants attention, the part that wants
everything to be under control, the part that craves
adventure, the part that is critical, the part that re-
sents demands . . . Make a list of your different selves,
then ask yourself the following:

— Which parts get the most opportunity for
  expression?
— Which get the least?

In a person with Me Phobia, the angry, self-centered, demanding self has usually been disowned or
driven underground early in childhood because the
message was given loud and clear that these responses were dangerous and might cause parental
disapproval or rejection. In an effort to be whole and
bring those parts of the self back, the pleaser often
hooks up with someone who has not disowned these
selves.

If you examine the things that you hate most about
your man, you will probably have a clue about which

parts of yourself you have disowned. Harville Hendrix, Ph.D., has developed an entire system of couples therapy based on this concept. He believes that this very connection—understanding the ways in which one person expresses the other's disowned self—contributes to the healing potential of even the most rocky relationships. (For information on Dr. Hendrix's methods, read *The Conscious Marriage: Getting the Love You Want from the Person You're With,* Henry Holt & Co., 1987.)

Now continue the exercise.

—Acknowledge the disowned parts of yourself. Give each one a blank page in your loose-leaf notebook and let it speak to you about how it feels and what it needs. The power of each of these unrecognized parts of you is directly related to how little attention you pay to it. In other words, by acknowledging your self-centered part, it will become more friendly and less likely to sabotage your life.

This is probably the most complex of all the exercises and that's why I left it until near the end of the chapter. It might take some practice to get the idea, but it will be worth the effort.

If you would like to learn more about this method of voice dialogue, read *Embracing Ourselves,* by Dr. Hal Stone (Devorss and Co., P.O. Box 550, Marina Del Rey, CA 90294)—Dr. Stone created this method of consciousness-raising.

Here is an easy exercise to finish up the recovery program.

16. Buy Time on Commitments

Start buying time to think about the requests that are made of you every day. For example, suppose your boss calls you into his office and asks, "Can you stay late tomorrow night to help me finish this report?" Instead of agreeing immediately, buy time. Say, "Let me get right back to you on that." Then go to a quiet place and decide in a methodical way whether or not you want or need to please him by staying late. This will give you the space to consider whether he is using you by taking advantage of your willingness to work long hours. You might reach the conclusion that it is time to say no for the first time. Or you might decide that tomorrow night is the perfect chance to score some points so you can ask for that raise next week.

In your notebook, write down the requests that are made of you on a daily basis for a week. Also note the things you do for others without their asking. Then jot down the occasions on which you bought time and what the result was—were you more apt to say no or do what you wanted to do when you thought first and then acted?

For every occasion when you bought time to think out your answer, put one dollar away and save up for something special that you already have in mind.

As you can see, the exercises I have given you cannot be done in one day, one week or even one month. They require an ongoing effort over a period of at least six months, although you will begin to see results right from the start. You will begin to feel that there is indeed something to *you,* something substan-

tial, and hopefully you will become hooked on looking more deeply into the well from which your being
springs. The longer you work on this notebook, the
more creative you will become with the exercises,
shaping them to meet the needs you find you want to
pursue further.

You will begin to conquer your Me Phobia. Until
now, as a pleaser, you have found yourself looking
for another person to tell you that you are okay. You
haven't taken responsibility for yourself. This is the
bottom line in your recovery: *you have the right to be
the final judge of your own behavior.* And you must
take the responsibility for deciding what works and
what doesn't. If others get angry, it's not the end of
the world. If others get anxious, it's not the end of the
world. *They are responsible for themselves.*

After the recovery process, you will feel like a different person. And now you have a new challenge:
how are you going to integrate this person of sub-
stance into the relationship you have with your man?
Or, if you are alone, how will this recovery influence
you as you look for a lover and companion?

The next and last chapter will address these issues
and help you—the new *you*—to be a happy and content member of a twosome.

11

LEARNING TO LOVE

Not long ago, I had a conversation with my friend Peggy. We had talked often in the course of my writing this book and Peggy had always expressed great interest in hearing about the conclusions I reached about conquering Me Phobia. When I first told her the premise, Peggy laughed and said instantly, "That's me, alright." About a year ago, she divorced her husband of five years and she told me then, "For the first time in my life, I'm determined not to be run by men. I want to find out what I want and who I am before I get involved in another relationship."

Like many women, Peggy had always defined the passages of her life through the men who were a part of each period. She had never taken that necessary time out to reflect about her own needs. She sensed, correctly I believe, that she needed time after her marriage ended to work on herself.

Now, more than a year later, as I prepared to complete the final chapter of this book, Peggy and I found ourselves talking about her personal journey to selfhood.

"I feel pretty good about myself," Peggy told me. "More in touch. And I've done things since I've been on my own that I never thought I'd be able to do. The night I handled the flooding toilet was quite a milestone for me." She laughed a little sadly. "I guess we don't need men, after all."

"That's not the point of my book," I reminded her.

"I guess I know that. But, for myself, I'm not sure how to have a good relationship with a man. I'm afraid that if I get too involved, the same bad situations will repeat themselves."

"You're a different person now."

"Yeah, but getting involved with a new man would certainly be the acid test, wouldn't it?"

"You seem to be afraid of trying," I told Peggy.

"I am," she agreed. "I'm afraid of two things. First, that I'll never meet the kind of man I can have a real relationship with—one that doesn't have all the manipulation and game-playing. And second, I'm afraid that if I *do* meet a really wonderful man at this stage in my life, I'll be so nervous about losing him that I'll fall back into the old patterns of living to please him."

"Pleasing doesn't work to keep a man," I reminded her gently. "You've learned that the hard way ... and you've come very far in learning to love yourself during the past year. The person you are now has much more likelihood of developing a truly loving, sharing relationship with a man than the old Peggy did."

"I agree," said Peggy. "But I also feel a little bit like

a recovering alcoholic. I have to take things one day at a time and I'm always aware of the danger that I might slip back into my old mode. I feel better about myself than I have ever felt, but self-discovery isn't an instant process. It seems as if I'll have to work on it every day of my life."

Like Peggy, you will find that the process of self-discovery is an ongoing one. And it is a path you will follow one day at a time for the rest of your life. You are and always will be a recovering Me Phobic.

But take heart because there is one very important change that has taken place inside you during the eight-step process: *For the first time in your life, you are ready to have a loving, equal relationship with a man.* You have traded in your old logic, "If I can meet his needs and please him, he will meet mine and make me happy," for the new, healthier logic, "If I can meet my own needs, I will make myself happy." You recognize that by becoming more independent and responsible for your own life, you have new choices available to you.

I'll even go so far as to suggest that your new motto might be, *"The only truly wonderful relationship is one that I can live without."* That's a radical thought, but you might even find it reassuring now that you understand that your only real security lies within yourself.

In this final chapter we will take a look at you and your relationships. You might have decided to stay in your relationship and change it. Or you might have left your controlling man and are on your own now, seeking a new relationship.

If you have chosen to stay, remember that your

recovery process from Me Phobia is not guaranteed
to improve your current relationship—it is meant to
make you a more complete person. It might even
cause you some new problems. Threatened by this
new you, your man might try to become even more
controlling. I hope you are strong enough to stay on
the course you have set for yourself and not give up.

Whether you are staying in your current relationship or you have decided to leave, you should take
seriously your need for support during this period.
You might want to turn again to the friend who
helped you do the exercises in Chapter Nine. If she
is a recovering Me Phobic, she will need your support, as well.

Here's another suggestion: *symbolize* your new
commitment to the process of knowing thyself by
buying yourself a special ring to wear on your right
hand. It doesn't have to be expensive but it should be
purchased with your own money. (Later in the chapter we'll talk about what you should do if you don't
have money of your own.)

Finally, write down some vows to yourself—and
take them as seriously as you took your wedding
vows, if you're married. The main purpose of this is
to promise to be true to yourself. Buy a special ring
to symbolize your commitment. Put it on your right
hand. You can do it with your supporting buddy or
alone, but having the ring on your right (or *dominant*)
hand should remind you constantly of your *dominant*
commitment to yourself. (Even if you're left-handed,
the act of creating a special ring finger will be an
important symbol for you.)

Now let's talk about the guidelines for a loving,
equal relationship. As we discuss each one, it will

become clear to you how loving is different from pleasing. The guidelines look like this:

L et go.
O bserve and give accordingly.
V alue your independence.
E stablish your credibility.

LETTING GO

Up until now, you have probably been taking the lion's share of the emotional responsibility in your relationships with men. You felt that if you didn't hold things together, who would? This has to change now because one of the first characteristics of a loving relationship is the equality of the commitment. *Both* of you have to care about what becomes of it and both of you have to work to make it mutually satisfying.

When you take *more* than half of the responsibility, you become the caretaker of the relationship and your actions are more characteristic of a mother than a lover. These motherly characteristics are:

— You feel anxious and responsible when your man has a problem.
— You anticipate his needs.
— You consistently abandon your routine when he needs or wants something.

— You feel bored or empty unless you can focus on
   him.

Even though your man might respond positively to
your mothering, believe me, it doesn't make him feel
good about himself. Instead, it simulates feelings of
weakness and powerlessness. Eventually, he comes
to resent you for being the caretaker.

If you relinquish the mothering role and let go of
your feelings of total responsibility for the relationship, you will both be free to develop a mutually
responsible relationship.

What does this kind of relationship look like? Here
are some of the ways you can identify a loving (as
opposed to a pleasing) relationship:

LOVING	PLEASING
1. The responsibility for the relationship is mutual.	1. One person's needs are secondary to the other's.
2. There is trust.	2. There is possessiveness and fear of being left.
3. You value your time apart. You're each secure inside.	3. Time apart is intolerable because security rests in acceptance from the other.
4. You say no when you mean no.	4. You try to be perfect and say yes even when you mean no.

LOVING	PLEASING
5. You encourage each other's growth and change.	5. You try to control the other person's change to meet your own needs.
6. You focus on personal growth.	6. You focus on maintaining security.
7. You give from the heart.	7. You give with strings attached or take gifts as bribes.
8. You take responsibility for your own happiness and success.	8. You take too much responsibility for the other person's happiness and success.
9. You primarily act for yourself, even though you have the other person's needs in mind.	9. You primarily react to the other person.
10. You want to love and be loved.	10. You need to be needed.

Letting go of your obsession with him should be a lot easier now that you have another important project to work on for the rest of your life—*you.* You will keep yourself productively occupied and you can relax and let others live their own lives. You can learn to love and care without giving up your own self in the process.

OBSERVE AND GIVE ACCORDINGLY

Giving is often the most difficult part of a relationship for a recovering Me Phobic. You're used to giving too much, giving with strings attached and giving to your man what you need for yourself. Now that you are no longer operating as a pleaser, you need to clarify what giving will mean to you.

The act of giving in a truly loving relationship is a magnificent testimony to the goodwill of mankind. It is an act that is tailor-made for the person who is the recipient. There are no strings attached.

How do you tailor-make an act of giving? Just as different countries have different currencies and you cannot be an effective shopper in France if you are using Italian lira, so too you cannot be an effective giver if you are giving him what *you* want. That seems logical, right? Yet many women never stop to think about what their men really want. As pleasers, we are constantly acting from the standpoint of our own insecurity. If we give him a lavish gift for his birthday, is it something he really wants or are we setting a precedent so that when our birthday comes around, he will respond in kind? Maybe he prefers not to get gifts on his birthday. We know it but we buy anyway. Why? Because we are thinking about what he is going to give back, not about the sanctity of our gift.

Sometimes when we try to be there for a man emotionally, we are really trying to give him the kind of support that would satisfy *us*. Maybe our man is having problems at work and we encourage him to talk about what's bothering him. Most men aren't particularly interested in sitting down for a long, intimate talk about the problems they're having at work. Because so much of their self-esteem is tied up in work, these discussions can lead to feelings of failure rather than lend the intended support.

You have to ask yourself, "What would really help here?" Maybe it's sex or some other form of non-verbal support. Many men will tell you that when they're troubled, there is nothing that makes them feel as cared for as making love and allowing passion to quiet their misgivings.

I'm not suggesting that you seduce your man if that's not what you want. I'm only suggesting that you be open to seeing what it really means to give support in your particular situation.

When you are feeling insecure about yourself in the relationship, you are engaged in a dizzying cycle of worry and fear that precludes your potential for intimacy and mutual support. Maybe you take all of his behavior too personally, assuming the focus is on you. If he gets angry, you think about what you have done wrong, rather than letting him experience his own feelings. (Don't forget that people can get angry and still love each other!) At the same time, don't assume that his silence necessarily means everything is alright—men often have trouble expressing their emotions. Overall, it is best to pay more attention to his deeds than his words.

One caller to my radio program plaintively asked me how she could get her husband of thirty-nine years to tell her that he loved her. She recited a litany of all the things he did for her on a daily basis, painting a picture of a man who was smart, loving, caring, considerate and responsible—and someone who had trouble expressing feelings of love.

I explained to her that many men are far more dependent on their marriages than their wives imagine, but they have trouble admitting this dependence, even to themselves. I asked her to stop trying to manipulate him into saying the words and, rather, let his actions speak for themselves.

"Yes, but isn't there anything I can do to get him to *say,* 'I love you'?" she repeated, obviously not having heard or understood what I was saying. I found it sad because, in trying to manipulate her man, this woman was missing out on the real experience of love.

VALUE YOUR INDEPENDENCE

The third characteristic of love is that each person must be separate individual, independent yet dependent. It's a state that might be called interdependence.

You have been learning throughout the eight steps of recovery from Me Phobia how to begin to see yourself as an individual, maybe for the first time. Now, as you either continue your relationship with the same man or seek a new relationship, it is important that you never forget who *you* are.

Unfortunately, power in our society is defined by money—and by that I mean *who makes it.* Women, especially pleasers, don't like to hear me tell them how important it is for their independence to have their own source of income. They are frightened of rocking the boat—"He'll be mad at me if I'm not there to cook dinner." Or they believe that there is nothing

218   BORN TO PLEASE

they can do that is of economic value—"What can I do that someone will pay me for?"

Even if you do not *need* to work to support yourself, it makes a difference when you are doing a job that has a financial return.

If you are not currently working, read on for some encouragement about making the move.

If you're scared about rocking the boat by starting to make your own money, remember that his reaction is based on being threatened by your independence. He might be afraid that if you can make it financially without him, you might leave him. He will try to change your mind about this, using his controlling tactics. Do you recognize them now—charm, guilt, threats? Reach through his anger and touch his fears. Let him know that this is the only way there is to *save* the relationship and encourage him to recognize that your independence is not a threat to him.

Here is an example of a dialogue that might give you an idea of how to approach your man about your need to get a job:

HELEN: I've been thinking about getting a job. The kids are busy with their lives and I have too much time on my hands.

GARY: I don't know ... the house looks like it could use three or four pairs of hands right now.

HELEN: You're right, but I guess I just really want to work.

GARY: You *do* work. You work here.

HELEN: [*sigh*] I want to get out more.

GARY: I don't understand why. This is where you belong. Didn't you agree when we got married that you'd always be here for me and the kids? How can you change your mind now and let us down? Besides, what would you do? You're not trained for anything.

HELEN: I've been thinking about that, too, but I'm still going to give it a try.

GARY: What about the extra expense we'll have hiring someone to do the things you won't have time to do?

HELEN: I know that will be expensive, but I have to start now.

GARY: It sounds to me like you're being pretty selfish.

HELEN: I am thinking about myself . . . and it feels good. It doesn't take away from my feelings about you and the kids.

GARY: That's what you say, but who will be here for them when they come home from school?

HELEN: I would like to be able to be there for them then. Maybe I'll be able to get a job where that will be possible. If not, we'll find a way to have them cared for . . .

And so on. Agree with the valid points he makes, but stay firm about what you want to do. See if you can discover why he is really so resistant to this change. Why is it so painful to him? Was he left alone a lot as a boy? Does he worry that people will look down on him as a poor provider? Is he afraid that you'll meet another man and want to leave him? Even when you understand his fear and reassure him about your love, be ready for the fact that he won't really start to feel better until you begin work and he sees firsthand that nothing terrible has happened. Do not get defensive or veer away from your goal. This is assertive behavior in the truest sense.

Now, what about your concern that you don't know what you could do in the workplace? Start looking through the classified ads in your newspaper and cut out every one that holds even a tiny bit of interest for you. Do this even if you feel you aren't qualified for the job. Arrange the ads in groups on large sheets of paper. You decide what the groups will be—home-based jobs, human services jobs, and so on.

Then put the sheets away and look at them every night, seeking patterns in what you might like to do and already have some experience doing, even if you've never been paid. Finally, pick out an area in which you can begin to get volunteer experience. I don't know of any area where a person cannot arrange to volunteer. In fact, I know a woman who volunteers at my radio station one day a week. Once your volunteer work is under way, you are building a résumé. You are getting important experience and you are meeting people who can eventually help you land a paying job. This process can be great fun and a real adventure.

To reaffirm your independence, you might also want to use your own name as much as possible. If you're married and have taken your husband's name, use Mrs. Louise Kaufman, for example, instead of Mrs. Bernard Kaufman. If you're not married, consider keeping your own last name when you do get married. You may ask, "What's in a name?" Your *identity* is in your name.

Sometimes you're going to be scared of behaving independently. You'll have moments of panic when you feel as though your links to happiness and security are being severed. You might think, "What will happen to me if I can't depend on him?" These feelings may never go away completely, but I promise that they will become overshadowed by the positive pride and exhilaration you'll feel about being your own person.

Remember, too, that your independence will allow a beautiful and nurturing relationship with a man. Let him get to know who you are; let him love you for being that person, not because you're focused on pleasing him. The rewards can be very great.

ESTABLISH YOUR CREDIBILITY

The important man in your life must take you seriously as an equal or your relationship is not worth its salt. That's true whether the man in question is a blind date or your husband of thirty years. Ask yourself this question and answer truthfully: "Does my man respect me?"

If your answer is no, face the painful fact that your man does not really love you.

Maybe you've never asked for or demanded respect and if that is so, this aspect of love might be hard for you to understand. You will need to begin by deciding how you want to be treated in a relationship—what is ideal, what you will tolerate and what you will refuse to accept.

To place your boundaries in perspective, make three columns on a sheet of paper. In the first column, list the characteristics of an *ideal* relationship. In the second column, write a realistic list of what is *acceptable.* In the third column, write the things that are *unnaceptable.*

MY RELATIONSHIP

IDEAL   ACCEPTABLE   UNACCEPTABLE

The last column will probably be the most difficult to complete—we'll call these your "boundaries." Think about how much you will do, how far you will go, how much you will take. Your "unacceptable" list may look something like this or it may be quite different:

- It is unacceptable for me to be physically or emotionally abused.
- It is unacceptable for me to be intimidated in my own house.
- It is unacceptable for me to be embarrassed in front of my friends.
- It is unacceptable for me to finance or lend support to another person's irresponsible or destructive lifestyle.
- It is unacceptable for me to always be the one who waits on others.

- It is unacceptable for anyone to spoil my day or my life.
- It is unacceptable for anyone but me to set my goals.
- It is unacceptable for my (or our) money to be spent in ways I am unaware of.
- It is unacceptable for anyone to criticize me in mean-spirited ways that are not justified by my behavior.
- It is unacceptable for me to be told that my opinions are not important.
- It is unacceptable for my point of view not to be considered.

This list of boundaries will be your day-to-day guideline for making certain that you don't slide back into being a pleaser. Stay firm about what you will accept and what you will refuse to accept.

Chances are you've had ideas about what your boundaries are, but in the past you've backed down when they were challenged because you were too frightened of the consequences of standing firm. Or you were so unsure of yourself that you questioned their validity. Or you just got used to constantly compromising. What you are really doing here is establishing the ground rules for your breaking point—how much you will and will not take. You're becoming clear in your own mind just what would have to happen to make you leave a relationship. And in the process you are also defining more clearly what for you is a good relationship. Don't back down. Your life and sanity are at stake.

Love is also at stake. The ability to stand up for

yourself is the only way you will ever be able to have a relationship based on love, not control.

As a recovering Me Phobic, you have always had trouble setting limits. You have been so busy pleasing others that you are not only unclear about how you want to be treated, but you are also extremely reluctant to try to get your way. It might be particularly troublesome for you to think about setting up consequences for the limits you establish ("I will leave you if you . . ."). Here are some principles that might help you:

1. Decide what the repercussions will be before an incident occurs. Don't act impulsively.
2. Make sure that you neither overreact nor underreact to the violation. An overreaction might be saying something like, "If you are late one more time, I will never cook dinner for you again." An underreaction might be saying, "If you flirt with a woman at a party, it will make me upset."
3. Make the repercussion specifically related to the violation.
4. Be certain that you can carry through with the repercussion and are willing to stand firm. Otherwise, don't even bring it up. You will lose more credibility if you can't follow through.
5. Tell your man clearly what is going to happen if the situation ever occurs again. Preface your statement with something positive about the relationship. For example, you might say, "I enjoy spending evenings with you watching TV, but I would enjoy them more if you weren't constantly asking me to bring you things from the kitchen. I

work all day and I'm tired in the evening. If you do ask, just be forewarned that I will not go more than once [or twice] in an evening." Or you might say, "I will bring you things when you ask, but I expect you to do the same for me."

6. Finally, make sure you ask him to tell you how he feels about what you have said. An equal sharing of feelings is important to establish honest dialogue.

Just a warning: Expect not to be taken seriously at first and to be tested more than once. Some men will be very threatened by your new assertiveness. Be on the lookout for the threat of physical violence and, if at any point you feel in danger, leave the situation.

STORIES OF SUCCESS

A friend of mine got fed up with her husband because he frequently came home late without calling first. Finally, she told him that she was not going to start cooking until she saw him walk through the door. She explained that she resented his being inconsiderate, especially since she worked too and cooking for him was something extra. He didn't like to eat late and after a few evenings of having dinner served around 10:00, he never again came home late without letting her know. Eventually she also began to encourage him to do some of the cooking himself.

This may seem like a very small victory for my friend, but it was an important step for her. By taking a firm stand on this issue, she established her credibility with her husband, and that carried over into other areas.

Another woman told me that her boyfriend always gave her a beautiful gift the day after he had behaved badly or embarrassed her in front of her friends—usually by openly flirting with another woman. She told him that she could no longer tolerate his behavior, nor could she accept his morning-after payoffs. The next time it happened, he bought her a new printer for her computer—something she really needed. But she stood firm, refusing his gift and gently reminding him of her previous statement. He was shocked by her refusal to accept such an expensive and much-needed gift, and he tried again the next week with the gift of a watch. Again she refused. Eventually he got the point and much of his outrageous and hurtful behavior stopped.

Sometimes the repercussions have to be more drastic. One woman, confronted with her husband's repeated affairs, told him she wanted a separation. "I can't be with you until you make a commitment to get counseling. I can no longer tolerate your affairs."

In other areas, where it is not so much a matter of his unacceptable behavior, but more an issue of your preferences, think more carefully about how you will deal with the situation, keeping in mind who he is and who you are. Don't make every issue an area for combat. Don't make every disagreement an opportunity for a power struggle. Most of all, except for keeping to your bottom line, don't let too much of the focus be on him. Keep working on yourself so you don't slip back into Me Phobia.

YOUR JOURNEY TO ENRICHMENT

LOVE . . .

L — Let go.

O — Observe and give accordingly.

V — Value your independence.

E — Establish your credibility.

You have now gone all the way from pleasing to loving. It's been quite a journey—the most important one of your life. I suspect that you now feel very different; fuller and happier, like a flower that has blossomed. You can say without reservation that you are beautiful, acceptable, worthy of love *just the way you are.* Your dark fears have evaporated in the light of your new understanding and your respect for yourself. I congratulate you on the journey you've taken and the growth you've achieved. Now you are prepared to have a different relationship with a man, one that is based on intimacy and sharing rather than on fear, power and control. Welcome to your new life!